Billy, the book

Billy-Luise Sauerampfer

BILLY,
THE BOOK

AN ATTEMPT TO UNDERSTAND
THIS WORLD

Bibliografische Information der Deutschen Nationalbibliothek:
This publication is listed in the Deutsche Nationalbibliographie of
the Deutsche Nationalbiblothek; detailed bibliographical
information can be accessed under dnb.dnb.de

Graphic: Pozdeyev Vitaly/ Shutterstock.com
Layout, cover design and publisher:
BoD · Books on Demand GmbH, In de Tarpen 42,
22848 Norderstedt, bod@bod.de
Printing and production: Libri Plureos GmbH, Friedensallee 273,
22763 Hamburg

ISBN: 978-3-7693-8568-7

CONTENTS

POEMS, RANTS, SERIOUSNESS, FURY,
AND HUMOR

FOREWORD

I've been journalling since I was 14.

The questions I've explored in my journals aren't new ones: Who am I? What am I here for? What's up with love? Why do I — like so many other people — have the feeling I still haven't found what I'm looking for? What am I looking for? Myself. But who is that?

I describe my search, my journey here — and if something in it rings a bell or strikes a chord with a reader, I'll have already reached my writer's goal: evoking an experience of suffering, or joy, or knowledge that we have in common.

The wars that are raging around the world are also raging inside me. For a long time, I was sick of the world, just as the world is sick of us human beings. I want to find peace and healing within myself. I'm getting there, though I stumble and make mistakes along the way. Without the mistakes, though, I wouldn't have anything left to learn. I'm a collection of quotes. Perhaps one day, someone will have fun quoting me.

The various peoples on our planet have different languages. Why shouldn't they also have different names for their gods? Why in the world do we fight about such tiny differences even though a common destiny unites us? The Earth is in a deplorably wretched state — and so are all the living beings that humans haven't already wiped out. I want to do something helpful that goes beyond picking up other people's cigarette butts and other litter.

Something that helps switch on a light in people's heads —and first and foremost in my own!

And I want to love! Within these pages, I want to show how the road to love can be rocky, but also beautiful.

INTRO

I want to get to know myself. I want to understand myself. I want to love myself.

What have I retained, what have I forgotten, or even repressed? Where have I been warped, surrounded, or entangled — and how am I developing now? Who is ME? People started calling me Billy when I was 18, and that's the name I've answered to ever since. It was time, I guess, to pick a name and stick with it before I drifted away in the flood of nicknames people called me: *Duckerchen* (little ducker), *Bienchen* (wee bee), *Spinette* (little loon), *Homi* (homie) *Omi* (granny), *Nettchen* (sweetie), *Annettchen*, (little Annette), and *Nettilein* (sweetie pie).

Different people think I'm a different person. Is my face so commonplace? Or: why do people often confuse me with somebody else?

Like Albert Einstein, I believe that nothing is lost in this world, that energies are transformed, that time is an illusion. C. G. Jung and his idea of the universal subconscious seems more plausible to me than anything I've ever heard about different gods.

Who is ME?

A nothing, a SOLITARY being, a teensy drop in the sea, a grain of dust from some ethereal space cloud, a fart let out by the world spirit or even a breath?

I feel like an old-timey radio with an antenna receiving different signals, sometimes this one, sometimes that one. So, I turn the dial and what I hear is a chorus of all the spirits I've summoned. As if everything that has been thought, is being thought, will be thought, is present in the ether and enters my mind at the right moment as inspiration, becomes a catchy tune, a song, a poem or even a picture.

Who is speaking through my mouth?

GOAL

In this book, I attempt to understand myself as being part of the whole but at the same time realizing and defining myself as a separate individual. I want to understand, to find the truth, the quintessence.

I'm quite aware that every human being experiences their very own reality and for each of us, truths emerge from how we perceive and subjectively interpret our sensory experiences. But hey, these are all just my opinions.

Or are they? I guess not since I know that sentences from other spirits bubble out of me that I've somehow internalized as fitting and true for me.

WHERE DO I COME FROM?

My parents met at the German University of Physical Education in Leipzig. They became teachers, moved in together, and got married.

Peter was born on January 7, 1964. I came along on January 4, 1967. My father, mother, brother, and I lived with my paternal grandmother in the same house.

My parents were both born in 1940, during WWII. My father's father was in combat, captured as a POW, seriously ill upon his release and return home, and died when my father was 17. Grandma tried to take her own life three times. My father saved her each time. I'm sharing this story first so you can understand why he became such a "tough guy," such a strict coach. I was given a special lesson very early on to awaken my self-preservation instinct. I must have been just over a year old at the time. My father took my little feet in his hand and pulled me backwards across the Baltic Sea on my stomach. At my mother's indignation, he reportedly said, "The little one will learn to keep her head above water." He must have scared me to death.

When I think of myself as a small child, I see myself, well, alone with my brother. He was the most important, the dearest to me, my friend, my protector. I wanted to marry him when I grew up. I always had to wait three days for my birthday until it was Peter's birthday too. Then we celebrated at the same time. One year, we received bathroom scales as a present and jumped around on them until they broke. The interesting thing is that he preferred my doll, and I got his toy cars. He was cautious, I was the wild one. I can see us playing in the attic outside father's study or in the garden, or in the living room melting plastic straws on the hot door of the wood burning stove. I burned my fingers once doing the latter. Peter must have been six years old and was clever enough to cut open a potato and press it on the painful spot. It helped. Partly because I believed him.

Then Peter got leukemia and was taken to the Charité hospital in Berlin. When he could come home for a visit, he was all bloated from cortisone, weak, and sad. He died in hospital in 1971. I was four years old.

His death heralded the beginning of the end of our family history. My mother plunged into deep mourning, while my father became more active than ever. They couldn't comfort each other. I only found out what had happened from my grandma. My parents went their separate ways. I was the child left over, and not the child that everyone was missing so much. I began to wish that I would die of cancer too. Then when they visited my grave, my parents would be sorry they hadn't paid attention to me.

I later learned that there was already a way to cure this type of cancer in the West. That's when I started to curse borders. Everything should be for everyone. I was alone, disappointed with the world and with people. This isn't supposed to be a book of whining — oh, poor me. No! Every crisis offers opportunities, and everyone has a cross to bear. I found solutions, created my own world, continued to talk to my brother in spirit, found friends in stones, plants, and animals. Nevertheless, I still took almost everything people tried to sell me as gospel truth. Almost! You say this is red and that's blue. How can I know whether the red I see isn't your blue?

When I was five, one of the oldest swimmers in our town promised me that I could have a donkey if I gave it a place to stay in our shed and agreed to take good care of the creature. Of course, I promised, and I did everything I could to make it happen. When I later announced that I was ready for the donkey to come, I was laughed at for being so stupid as to believe the grown-ups. Shocked with disappointment, I said: "You're all hollow birds." Adults are people you can't trust. They do other things than what they say — and don't say what they think. Who knows what they really think. In any case, they say a lot of irrelevant stuff that has nothing to do with them or me.

In my world, blue isn't just blue, it's number five, and the color of the sky and the sea — it brings me a kind of bliss. I can think for myself what I want to. I'm just different. Death is relative. Truth is what I perceive it to be.

At night, I'd meet my brother. Like this: I fall asleep, dream that I get up, and go to the window of the room we shared as kids. I can already see him coming along the garden path, he steps beneath the window so that we can see each other clearly. Eye to eye and not a word is spoken. We just look at each other and everything is clear, was clear, and will be clear.

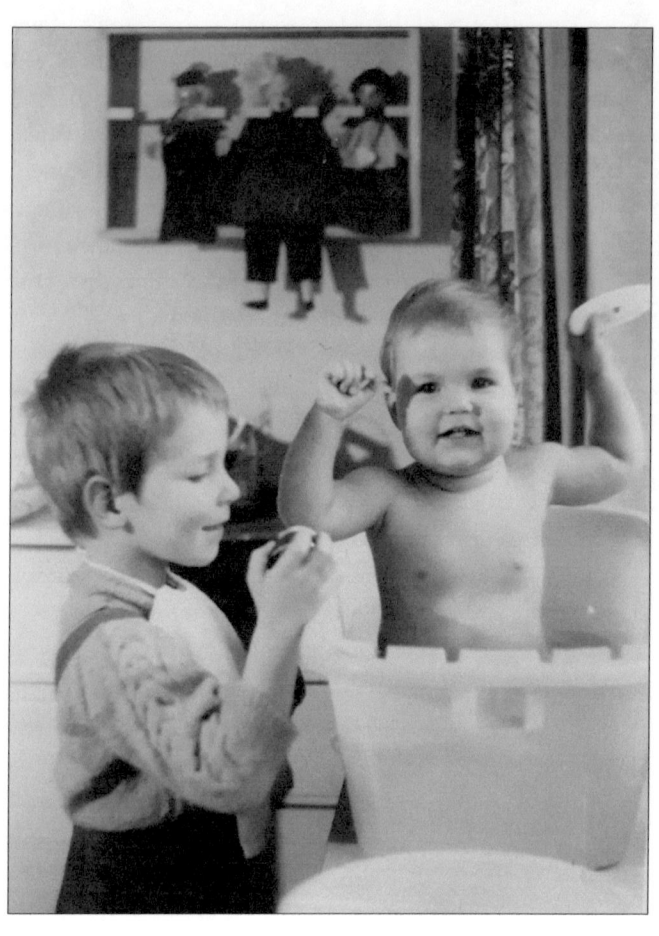

MAKE YOUR OWN LUCK

When it comes to making your own luck (and happiness), I didn't exactly have the easiest path for learning how to do it. I was five or six years old when one of my mother's singing partners, who was also a gifted pianist, ended up drunk in my bed. He did things to me there. The poet's politeness is almost silent. A big hand over my mouth and nose, shortness of breath, trapped under the covers, claustrophobia, and a huge cock in my hand. Shock, shame, disgust, revulsion! And of all people, I liked him so much because he seemed to understand how I was feeling with his sad Russian melodies. Or was just as sad as I was. How do you reconcile that? As a child, not at all, and I'm still working on it.

My brother and protector was dead, but not dead to me. I kept on talking with him about "life events," but likely was also repressing them and acted as if nothing had happened. To get ahead of myself here: In the rest of my life, I 've repeatedly found myself in similar situations. Favorite people turned out to be the worst.

Back then, I wanted to be nice, so I didn't let on. My father taught me: "No pain, no gain." In the morning, before he taught school, he would drive me to the swimming center. He'd make me swim the 50-meter course while he sat at the finish line holding a stopwatch. I was never fast enough for him, even though I got better and better. A coach, an alarm clock to awaken ambition. At that time, he called me "wee bee". Maybe because I was so busy and always humming to myself.

Soon, I got another coach and swam in the training pool at the elementary school that I was enrolled in starting at age six.

Lessons, training, new people. There were also flute lessons. I was kept busy.

"You were always the good child," my mother still says today. Unobtrusive, not a burden.

I talked with EVERYTHING, with rocks, little animals. When somebody misplaced or lost something, I just called to it by its name. Quite often, I found baby birds that had fallen out of their nests, or other creatures that needed help. I took them home to care for or nurture back to health and then set them free again. I know how to get birds to fly.

Sometimes my love of animals did not go as planned. For example, I once put some frog eggs into a jar, brought them to my room, and excitedly watched them develop. When they had passed the tadpole stage and turned into little frogs, I made a "natural" habitat — a baby bath with water and enough soil to create land. One day after my morning at school was done, I brought a friend home with me to show him the splendid wonder on my windowsill. We walked across the black and white carpet towards it, only to find when we got there, that most of the tiny frogs had escaped. Even worse, we had trampled some of them to death while crossing the room. Oh no! We collected the survivors and took them to a real natural habitat.

A born helper who only occasionally overdid it.

Love can be life-threatening.

I was given a parakeet and named him Bubi. Right from the get-go, Bubi was allowed to fly around the house as he pleased, had a large branch in my room, and a cage for his dining room and bedroom.

When water was running in the kitchen, he would come flying in. And if you cupped your hands together and filled them with water, Bubi liked to bathe in this "mini-tub."

By the way, my father, the bird and I whistled the same

way. When you heard a whistle, you never knew who was making it.

After one of these bird baths, I noticed that Bubi didn't fly when he was wet. He'd just sit calmly on my shoulder. I wanted to show this feat to the world, so I went out to the street and demonstrated to anyone who cared to see how loyal Bubi was to me. What I hadn't thought about, though, was that the little fellow would dry out. When he did, he simply flew off onto my neighbor's large lime tree. Dad got a ladder, and we used it to climb into the tree branches, whistling and coaxing. The higher we climbed, the further up the tree the precious parakeet went too, until we could no longer follow him. Three days later, we learned that Bubi had landed on a parrot cage that was on someone's windowsill. We were allowed to pick him up. Another lucky escape.

Whenever there was the sound of something splashing, Bubi came flying to check it out. This occurred during a musical soirée my mother was holding with some friends in our living room. The bird started drinking vodka, flitting from glass to glass, sipping here and there until it lost all inhibitions. Bubi sang his heart out and shared his entire repertoire.

His end was tragic. I was sitting at my desk, facing the wall, with the large branch behind me that was by then serving as Bubi's take-off ramp. From there, he flew straight into the wall and fell right down onto my homework. How come?

He was still alive, but the lower part of his beak had broken off and was hanging loose. The vet didn't give me any hope, still, he did give Bubi some vitamin drops just to do something at all. Death came promptly and relieved his suffering.

My school days ... I was seven when my parents divorced. For me, it was mainly a relief. I didn't have to listen to any more arguments. My father moved out and my mother stayed in the house with me and my grandma.

I soon acquired a puppy — a white Spitz. I'd lied to the previous owner and said my parents wouldn't mind. Basically, I presented my mother with a fait accompli.

"No way, what are you thinking! Take that dog back to where you got it from!"

And then in the next sentence:

"Oh, give it to me, it's so adorable." Since my mother was a Gemini, she could change her mind in no time flat. Wonderful! Now I had a creature that was important to me that I could look after. Unfortunately, just not for long.

I don't remember how old I was when I came home from summer camp and my mother told me: "Your dog has been run over, but she's still alive."

I found out what that meant a bit later. The vet's diagnosis was: Trolli had a concussion. I dared to hope that everything would be okay. I'd just completed a first aid course and decided I'd stay home with Trolli while my mother was at school teaching. A terrible drama. I watched this miserable suffering for hours and couldn't do anything to make it better. Sometimes the end was near, silence in the room, then I gave Trolli artificial respiration, and she lived on a little longer, howling, screaming, and agonizing. Blood ran out of her poor ears. If I had been smarter, I'd have realized her skull was fractured and not prolonged her suffering.

Brother dead, bird dead, dog dead, and not to forget, the baby frogs!

Was it my fault that the ones I loved so much all left me?

Then I got a new dog: Mr. Lehmann, also known as Trolli.

At night I kept communicating with my brother, during the day I was in this world with school friends, in the afternoon three times a week in the swim training group. There were competitions at the weekend. This went on until I was 12.

My father sometimes spent parts of the school vacations with me. Once we cycled to the High Tatras, a hundred kilometers a day. When I was 12, I confided in my mother about the assault in my early childhood. Her only response: "You're crazy!"

From that moment on, I stopped being the good child. From then on, I stopped being the good kid. My self-imposed guilt gave way to anger. I quit listening to love songs on AFN — the American Forces Network — and switched to AC/DC. At age 13, I lied about going to the movies with a friend and then sleeping over. In reality, I stole alcoholic drinks from my mother and grandmother, mixed them in a jar and drank them with my girlfriends. Then we'd go out to the disco together.

Life is change. This was the start of a revolt, also known as puberty.

WHAT I'VE LEARNED SO FAR

Life is cruel. The first event in this "movie" of my life was my birth. I can't remember it. But since it happened to me, I've given birth to two children myself. So, I think my own birth must have been a trauma. Out of the safe space, out of the warm womb. The being who had been giving me this nice home, is now screaming in pain. And later, you look around and try to feel safe in this family and build trust.

Yet, trust can be life-threatening. My father taught me that when he pulled me backwards through the waves as a baby. Violence from a loved one seemed okay. Why did my father call me "Duckerchen" (little ducker)? Maybe because I made myself extra small, kept myself subdued and inconspicuous so I wouldn't be noticed, and not be in danger.

Loved ones leave you, even if you think you need them.

In the meantime, my father had apparently found a new wife and another child.

Families aren't indestructible, members are replaceable. Death isn't the end. Eight years after my brother died, I was still talking with him.

Those who please others and ignore their own needs are nice. Here's the story. I must have been about seven. Mother had a visitor in the living room next door. I had already been ordered to go to sleep but couldn't because I was being plagued by a hellish earache. It was a middle ear infection, as it turned out later. I didn't dare ask for help for two reasons: "No pain, no gain." And: "Children are to be seen and not heard." By then I had learned enough to live up to my name Annette. (In German, "*nett*" means nice and kind.)

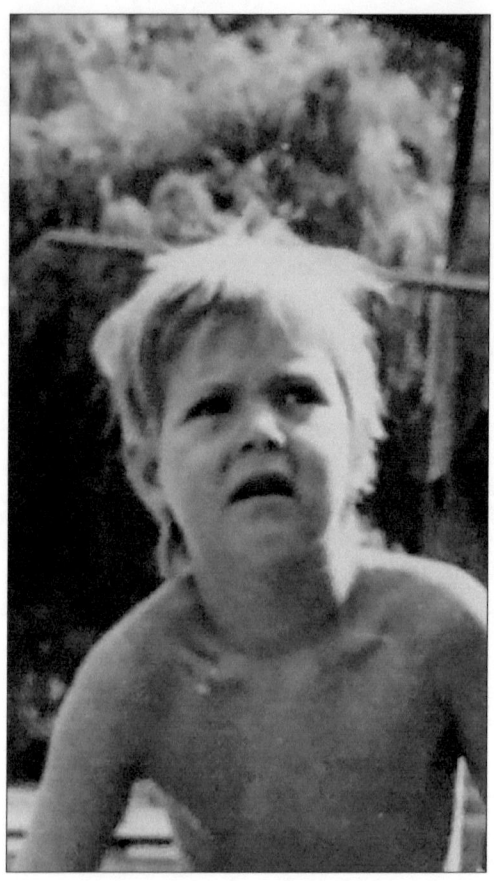

MORE STORIES

The timeline here leaves a lot to be desired, forgive me. I'm always going back to a particular time because other memories from it keep occurring to me.

After my father moved out and I became the man of the house, I shoveled tons of coal into the cellar, swept the yard, the stairwell and the 64 steps as a matter of course.

I was a good child and hard-working. Of course, I wanted to please everyone so that I'd be valued.

I'd learned that you can win recognition through athletic performance, hard work and cautious behavior.

Shortly after I turned 13, I stopped "chatting" with my brother. Crisis!

I didn't like being so alone at all. So, I put out feelers to see if there might possibly be a boyfriend for me here on earth.

For one whole summer — at a vacation camp — I had a crush and was his "squaw." At that time, attraction meant constantly thinking about each other but doing nothing beyond the innocent batting of eyelashes.

At age 14, I landed my first boyfriend via glances exchanged in the school stairwell and a note with a tender message that I gave to a friend of his: "Shall we go to the movies together?" I was lucky. The person I was interested in was also interested in me. We went for rides on his Simson S 50 motorbike and danced closely entwined to John Lennon's "Woman." Maybe I was trying more to find my brother in him. But with his awakening instincts, he was on the lookout for a female to get physical with. Poor guy! It didn't go well, and I broke up with him. I particularly remember the following passage from his farewell letter: "And every time I wanted to kiss you, mosquitoes were biting you or something else got in the way.

Just, everything wasn't like in the fairytales ("... and then they recognized each other and lived happily ever after") of my dreams. I held back for a long time. I liked being a good friend and only wanted to give my virginity to the one person I would stay with forever.

I also had my mother's advice in my head: "Men only want one thing. You can get pregnant the first time. Abstinence is the best birth control."

I split up, found the next guy who wanted sex and split up again.

I got my first period when I was 14.

LEAVE THE GDR?

My mother applied to leave East Germany, and I had to "bleed" for that decision at other levels. I'll never forget what it was like when our principal came to our class. "As you may already know, Annette's mother has applied to leave the country. It goes without saying that the state no longer supports people like that."

I became a hot potato. Anyone who wanted to get a place at a university or move up in the world at all figured it would be better to avoid being around me. Once again, I was treated as if I had done something wrong or shameful. But what had I done? I was the child of a mother who while hitchhiking, had fallen in love with a man who worked at the UN in the water and energy sector. He was a diplomat and that's why my mother was accused of espionage. What a misjudgment of the situation! These two people simply loved each other. As a result, the State Security Service picked me up for interrogation. They shined a glaring, blinding light into my eyes. My mother had already prepared me: "Just play dumb." I could manage that.

Many people shunned me, and I had to be vigilant about not saying anything hostile about the State in public. I continued living my life, though. I dutifully went to school. I trained, frolicked with friends at the gravel pit, and spent my summer vacation at the Baltic Sea like every year. I also fell in love again — and again. But I always took off as soon as anyone tried to get into my pants. Either I broke up or got dumped. Fortunately, we don't have to examine all that in detail.

LIFE BACK THEN

What I was thinking was: There must be more to life than this. Birth, nursery school, kindergarten, school, training, work at the same job for the rest of your life, get married, have kids, and after you retire, look after your grandkids — or head straight for a retirement or care home. Not an enticing prospect. It's all so strictly structured to keep you on the straight and narrow. However, being a child of divorce had convinced me early on that I was never going to marry anybody. Even back then, though, the scenes in movies where soulmates finally found each other made me cry. They still do.

I also really hated hearing about the vast, wide world out there in geography class since I knew we were locked up in this little country. And not just that! It was obvious that we were being watched and spied on. And you knew practically anybody would rat you out to the Stasi just for making a political joke — in return for a spot at a university or some other benefit. It wasn't just our freedom of movement that was restricted. It was also forbidden to think or speak freely.

This meant people had to adopt two mindsets, the state-sanctioned one and their own. You can imagine how this affected the way people treated each other. You had to choose your friends very carefully. (Careful! Big Brother is watching you!)

On the other hand, there were also many good things in the GDR. We always had enough to eat. When people lacked this or that, they bartered. "Hey, have you got a used car tire? I'll give you a pound of western coffee for it and regardless, you have my help anytime." It was a bit like the idea of communism: everyone according to their abilities, everyone according to their needs. I need something you have. In return I'll help you with what you need. The question remains, if everyone had everything and needed nothing and nobody, where would we end up? Maybe it would be wonderful. We could treat each other well out of pure affection. We'd be done with envy, no more dependencies, no fear of loss, no jealousy, no violence, and no war.

But that immediately gives rise to the next question: What do we humans actually need? The answer: no more than any other animal species does. We are all animals, just humans are supposedly gifted with reason! Humans need a safe home, food, water, and a companion. One who values and respects them, and also has the desire to let down their guard in the name of love and "make contact." That might lead to a love between two people that turns a YOU and ME into a WE where potentially, a child would be able to nest and flourish.

Am I getting sidetracked?

WHAT DO PEOPLE NEED?

And what can I do for the world? Right now, not a thing except look at my own self and try to understand where my weaknesses and strengths are.

One thing you can say about East Germany is: the State definitely took care of children. Talents were recognized and encouraged, whether in languages, music, sports or whatever. I was taught the flute, had piano lessons, learned Russian in the third grade, and sang in the school choir. I also learned to play table tennis and was briefly active in a handball club. Dryland swim training at the club included playing soccer. Today, I still prefer all kinds of activities that make you physically exert yourself. I don't like games that require sitting at a table. Nor do I enjoy watching other people play games or do sports while, for example, hanging out in front of a screen with a crate of beer for company and wearing a tracksuit for a sporty touch.

The state also made arrangements for vacations. If a child's parents didn't have time for a family vacation, the children were sent to training or vacation camps.

When I was 16, I joined the Society for Sport and Technology and got a motorcycle license that cost 3.50 East German marks a year. I also joined a carnival dance troupe — a so-called "*Funkengarde.*" This gave me a legitimate excuse for my nighttime excursions. Imagine, at that age I was required to be home at 10:00 p.m., while my girlfriend, who was two years younger, was allowed to stay out until midnight. There had been trouble about this "must be home by time" ever since I'd turned 13. I was already in the habit of going to discos. There were plenty in our area back then. It was a time when someone who wanted to dance, could still choose someone and politely ask them: "May I please... or shall we dance first?"

People, I even went to dancing school. That was considered "good form." I learned the waltz, Charleston, foxtrot, cha-cha-cha, and more. At prom, I saw my father tipsy for the first time. It was funny to see the boss out of control for a change.

When I look back on it today, I think, wow, what an active life it was. I took final exams when I was 16 and did quite well. My strategy was the day before an exam, I'd buckle down and write out the quintessence of the material being tested. I learn best when I'm writing. It slows down my thinking and the message has time to worm its way into my brain.

FUTURE?

Since I was very interested in rocks, I wanted to become a geologist. I aimed for admission to the college prep path in Germany's school system so I could do the so-called "Abitur." Abitur scores determine whether you can study at university or not. However, I wasn't allowed to do it. All my applications ended in one rejection after another. It was clear that the reason was because of the request to leave the country. I was lucky that a company took pity on me and let me start an apprenticeship as a textile worker.

Up to then, I'd been a committed swimmer. My West German connections became a career obstacle for me, though, and I was denied admission to a sports school.

My father comes to mind. He would have loved to have been world champion in something or seen his children fulfill this dream for him vicariously. He conquered his world with flying colors on many levels, only in the end he never felt that he'd got the recognition he thought he deserved. I can still see him in my mind's eye in front of the TV in the care home he was in, surfing through the channels trying to find one showing a tribute to him. What a shame. Alzheimer's had already messed with his head. By age 17, I'd mastered my apprenticeship curriculum so well that I was offered the chance to take the exam earlier. But the ever so well-informed Father State once again threw obstacles in my path. Then suddenly, after my mother had been pulling out all the stops for two years, we were finally allowed to leave the country. She had contacted Amnesty International, and an attorney called Mr. Vogel. Their efforts (including perhaps a bribe or two) likely led to our release.

EXPULSION

I was at work in the textile factory at the time, supervising three looms, knotting torn threads, and making other repairs. I had to be careful, jumping back and forth between the looms and ideally anticipating problems before they happened. It was loud at work, but I had found a way to deal with the noise. I danced to the rhythm of the machines. The boss caught me red-handed and chewed me out. "What do you think you're doing? How dare you just dance around here like that? What kind of work ethic is that?"

To the point! On August 20, 1984, two guys from the Stasi showed up at the textile factory. They flanked me left and right and led me out of the company, taking great care to ensure that I had no contact with any of my colleagues. They took me all the way home. There they instructed us to leave the country the next day and forbade us to tell anyone anything. We were summoned again that afternoon so that we could be ceremoniously released from our GDR citizenship.

I had no choice. Apart from the repressive aspects of the East German system, I'd been living a good life in my home. I thought I'd found the love of my life, had great friends, and could go dancing for as long as I wanted. I had given up swim training. I was gladly going skinny-dipping in the quarry pond.

I would lose everything, my father, my grandmother, my dog, friends, my home. And it looked like I was saying goodbye forever.

August 21, 1984: At 3:24 p.m., my mother, my 15-years

younger half brother, and I left the East German town of Finsterwalde and everything that had stood for home until then.

Before we left, I visited my best friend. We found "Fame — The Road to Fame" on TV, dreamed of never-ending times, laughed, cried, and got wasted.

On the way to the reception camp in Giessen, we had to change trains at the Frankfurt/Main central station. We passed by a fruit stand and my mother and I just freaked out. All these colors, fruits, and vegetables that we'd never seen before.

UPROOTED AND TRANSPLANTED

The sudden switch from East to West was bizarre. In the East, red slogans on giant banners were still adorning the land and cityscapes. "Together for our socialist fatherland and against imperialism." In contrast, Western ideology expressed itself with: "Marlboro. The great freedom." Hunky guy sits a horse, a desert in the background, smokes a cigarette, and is instantly free from all worries.

What nonsense! So, the people were being dumbed down here too. Only somehow more vividly. After Giessen we reached Schwaikheim in Swabia, a small town that was much quieter than Finsterwalde. My first friends in a foreign country were Turkish boys.

Turkish boys who taught me how to play pool.

My mother was still in charge and thought that I should try again to do the Abitur now that we were in this land of unlimited opportunities. That way, I could become "somebody" or "something" after all. I was almost 18 when I entered 10th grade and felt very out of place. The good thing was that I was allowed to go on a school trip to Edinburgh — my very first experience of traveling in the West.

As my mother didn't enjoy being in Swabia either, we moved to West Berlin. We stayed with a pastor friend in his large apartment in Wedding. Here I worked as a cleaner for the Easter parish. We soon found our own apartment on Hansaplatz and I tried again to become something "proper." I applied for an apprenticeship as a foreign language secretary.

Once more, I felt like I didn't belong. The girls around me were wearing make-up, dressed smartly, and so different from me. I made an effort anyway. It was only when I came down with various ailments that I allowed myself to give up this apprenticeship "for personal reasons."

GROWN-UP

I was 18 years young in West Berlin. The first place I checked out the dance floor was at "The Sound" in the Kurfürsten Street. I was amazed when I noticed that many people were dancing on their own. One guy even danced in front of a mirror — all in love with himself. Different countries, different customs.

I made friends and moved out of the apartment shared with my mother and little half-brother and into a two-room one in Moabit. I shared it with four guys who all lived in rather questionable circumstances. My poor mother visited me after three months and was horrified to discover that I had "fallen off the wagon." Our everyday life was not rosy back then. We donated blood to get money and ate the drug Captagon to keep hunger at bay and dance until late in the night.

How my mother would have loved to have taken me under her wing again. She thought I had lost my way. But I got my act together by myself!

DREAM REALIZATION

I still had the idea in my head of seeing the world, of striving for a special life.

I worked as a waitress in the music café "Memory" in the Birkenstraße. I had a colleague at the bar but had to prepare and serve small meals for guests in both the indoor and outdoor seating areas by myself. And of course, cash up. This multi-tasking generally meant stress.

Things got really wild when the soccer World Cup was on TV. The café was bursting at the seams. The guests couldn't be served quickly enough and complained. This caused our boss, a little Turkish man, to give us hell, yell, rant, and try and motivate us by being nasty to us so we'd work even harder. The colleague at the bar burst into tears one day, threw in the towel, and vanished — never to be seen again. I was then supposed to perform a miracle and do everything on my own. That was impossible, so I left, too.

I'd been earning good money, so I called the carpooling center to see if anyone was heading for the sun, beach, and sea. I found a woman who was going to Naples. Along the way, she told me about a place she said had been made for me. "Freaks" from around the world meet up there. Travelling by train and ferry, hitchhiking, and bus, I reached a beach where I immediately felt at home. The people there were musicians and other creative folks from the States, England, Poland, Italy, Holland, Belgium, Austria, Germany and, of course, Greece. I had a small guitar with me and learned my first song:

"House of the Rising Sun." I realized that you can also drum on a guitar. Until then, I had only drummed on tables or my thighs.

At some point, a dozen percussionists of different nationalities and temperaments were sitting in a circle around a fire. Of course we sounded horrible at first. Many didn't know that the first rule of the road can also be applied to music: Caution and mutual consideration. First listen to understand when and how you can do your bit to enhance the sound.

BERLIN

Back in Germany again, I moved out of the five-person shared apartment and into my boyfriend's studio in the same building. In the meantime, two of the former roommates had made profitable contacts of a special kind: they had married two Thai girls and opened a small brothel. I became friends with the girls and was soon given the task of translating the customers' wishes and the ladies' conditions. I became the madam, so to speak.

At least I had work, but worried about people finding out about it. I'm imagining a family Christmas dinner right now:

"Well, Annettchen, Tell me, child, what are you doing for a living these days?" My maternal grandmother was very prim, proper, and prudish. The slightest off-color joke offended her. As a woman with an engineering degree, she set great store on making a good impression. I tried to avoid family gatherings.

I was still missing something in my life with this boyfriend and fortune sent a puppy my way. I brought him home and was beaming with joy, but my boyfriend wasn't thrilled. He said I wouldn't be allowed to come back to the apartment until I'd gotten rid of the dog. I wandered around the city for hours that day, talking to complete strangers, and hoping for help. I went to several pet shops and finally, the owner of one of them took pity on me. Of course I wasn't happy, but at least I still had a roof over my head.

Shortly thereafter, it dawned on me that I'd rather have my own apartment with a dog than live together with this boyfriend. When I'd first met him, I thought it was great that his dreams were similar to mine. Over time, though, I realized that he wasn't doing anything about realizing them. That's why I'd gone on that journey without him. It was for his sake that I'd come back at all. It was back when the Chernobyl reactor accident had just happened and there was a certain amount of panic about the resulting cloud of radioactive particles.

I was still a virgin and had been making my boyfriend wait because I wasn't sure about him. More than a year passed. He then had sex with someone else and I broke up with him.

THE FIRST TIME

I was out dancing in some dive when I saw a young man, thought I recognized him, and approached him. He thought that was funny because I'd used his standard pick-up line. He was with two friends. We danced, drank, and laughed. I felt like I was in good hands. Later, he invited me to come along and continue the party. He drove the car. His friends sat to the left and right of me in the back seat. They started touching me, which made me very uncomfortable. He called them off. In the apartment, I made it clear that I favored him. I already had the hots, but I explained at length that he wasn't allowed to go any further than a certain point, that I was still a virgin, and wanted to wait for the right guy. He agreed and led me to his bed.

He was French and quite obviously deaf to my NO, penetrated me, and I bled like a pig. Then he let go of me. Apart from the shock, I was terrified of being pregnant.

Change of subject.

I turned to the unemployment office, got a part-time job in the laundry at the Karl Bonhoeffer Mental Hospital, and my first apartment on my own.

After the deflowering, I had another go with my ex, this time with sex. But that didn't make our relationship any better. I tried motivating him to get his act together, find a job, and then realize his dreams together with me. But it wasn't to be. He didn't finally begin an apprenticeship until we'd split up again.

I really liked my work in the "loony bin." In the mornings, I'd meet the cleaning crew. They'd comment on my race against the

clock: "Get going, hurry up, you're already two minutes late!"
Being late or racing to catch trains runs in my family's blood.

GONE TO THE DOGS

I had a good job and my own apartment and soon got word that a dog in the neighbor's shed had been overwhelmed with a litter of 11 puppies. I went to check it out. The pups were just 10 days old. I made my choice instantly: I wanted the smallest, the puniest dog. It was hardly getting any milk but not old enough to be separated from its mother. A few days later I came by again and noticed that my chosen one still had no chance of being properly nourished. Its stronger siblings were hogging the source. So, I took the puppy home and fed it everything an animal needs: Oatmeal gruel from a bottle and lots of attention.

This dog probably thought I was its mother and training it was no problem. I got a pair of slippers that looked like little dogs and walked around the block wearing them. The puppy followed me. And when I noticed that it was getting distracted and not paying attention, I hid so that the dog would learn to keep an eye on me. Good method! This way I didn't need a leash, we had our own bond.

At first Grobi (as I called her) didn't make a sound, So I crawled around on all fours and barked. But no matter what I did, Grobi kept quiet. It was only when I played the guitar that she started to sing, and I found that the notes even matched. And when I played the harmonica, she howled like a wolf.

BONNY'S RANCH

Bonny's Ranch is the nickname of the Karl Bonhoeffer Mental Hospital.

Since I still hadn't completed my vocational training and had a certain sympathy for the "crazy," I applied to train as a nurse in the psychiatric ward. Funnily enough, I encountered one of my friends among the patients. He'd had a bad trip.

I'd been lucky, or rather made the right move when I took my life into my own hands. Lots of people I'd met in the West were already so in debt at a young age that anything resembling freedom was a distant prospect for them. They'd leased a car or TV, owned it on credit so to speak, and couldn't pay the installments. Additional charges and interest were added, dragging them ever deeper into debt. Was this a method the system used to make people toe the line?

Personally, I'd never been in debt. It just wouldn't have felt good, like having unfinished homework. I wanted to be free, explore the world, and spend as much time at the seaside as possible. I dreamed of perhaps being on the road in a camping van with my best friends, preferably musicians, finding the most beautiful places, and making a living from music. "There are dreamers. There are radicals. And there are radical dream realizers." I wanted to be the latter.

On my 21st birthday, I had a bird of paradise tattooed onto my left shoulder so that I'd always remember what I'm all about: finding idyllic places that were little paradises and living an extraordinary life. My apprenticeship alone was anything but ordinary.

SO CRAZY

My first practical work assignment took me to a closed psychiatric ward. Some of the patients had been living there for decades, one since the Second World War. Back then, he had been castrated — through use of two bricks.

I'll never forget my first day on the job. Six o'clock in the morning, the doors open, there's loud calling out, "Wake-up, get out of bed, go off to wash." What was I supposed to do? I was sent to a bathroom where three people were sitting on a bench, one woman and two men, all naked. The tub was full. It made me feel uncomfortable. I couldn't assess the situation. Just don't look like you're scared!

The woman was rocking back and forth. I thought to myself she must feel so uneasy and strange sitting naked between these two naked men. I suggested she get into the tub, took her hand, and guided her while I tried to calm her (and myself) down: "The warm water will do you good ..." She was rocking again in the water, but increasingly more calmly, while I murmured to her.

I'd just started thinking, the two of us are going to get along fine now. When suddenly, she stood up and scratched my face from top to bottom with all 10 fingers. How wrong can you be?

I left this challenging situation and was allowed to go to the in-house doctor. He treated me with some ointment and 10 band-aids. That looked lovely! Then he sent me back to work. In the meantime, the patients had been washed and dressed. I was sent to them in the room where they were to be kept occupied with various crafts and activities.

When I arrived, I got some paper and paint and then began creating. Immediately, a crowd of patients gathered around me. One of them started picking the lint off my cardigan and wouldn't let go of me. I was a real eye-catcher with my many bandages. One of the patients promised to protect me in future and told me to make sure I always had my back to a wall and never to show any fear. I had already thought of that, but my fear wasn't so easy to hide. You could smell it!

Over time, I made friends among the patients, including Jesus and Napoleon. I got on well with the people under my care — as long as I accepted everyone as who they thought they were. Some of my colleagues, on the other hand, had grown hardened. The tone of voice they used didn't make for nice music: "Get out of bed! Off to the bathroom!" No wonder that first woman I'd tried to help had been so unsettled by my gentle words and gestures. I was more drawn to those who were "outside the norm" and tried to empathize, to lure people out of their shells, to bring a smile to their faces.

One woman was plagued by contractures — a restriction of joint mobility. She lay curled up like an embryo in her bed. Even when she was turned onto her back, she remained in this position. I was told that she wasn't talking. I fed her and encouraged her every day with the same words: "Food will hold your body and soul together."

This went on for months until she suddenly replied: "Some people even eat it!"

Yeah! I had reached her. She had spoken.

The man who had been castrated during the war also didn't talk. He had the habit of knocking back any drink he could get his hands on. Interestingly, his name (that I must keep confidential) meant about the same thing as "bottoms up."

He always sat at the same table in a long corridor. Once, I

waited until he'd calmed down after a coughing fit. I walked backwards away from him but without breaking eye contact. When I was far enough away, I got a running start, did a cartwheel, landed right in front of him, and bowed. Man, what a laugh he had! And then he said,

"You're so crazy, you belong in a mental institution. Ha-ha."

He was right. I didn't feel normal either. What is normal?

Keeping up appearances or pretending that we're all exactly alike?

One thing's for sure: The inmates in this mental hospital were honest! Feelings were shown.

THE WORLD
AND ITS ILLS

We'd already gotten used to AIDS by then. In 1990 and 1991, when I was 23 or 24 years old, we had only just digested the reactor accident in Chernobyl. All of us would be getting cancer was the word at the time. Nature was already in dire straits. I was very worried. Then came the first Gulf War against Iraq.

But back to my work. I had completed my training, knew the craziness, had learned that every action has its reasons and its consequences. I had seen people die, washed corpses, and had a taste of all the medical fields practiced at the hospital. I realized that they only worked on the body, not the whole person. Each individual part was treated by a different specialist.

I once experienced the following in an intensive care unit: A homeless man was admitted. He had been dead for almost 10 minutes before he could be resuscitated. As a trainee, I had the dubious pleasure of caring for him. There were no relatives, no one who could have spoken on his behalf. And so I washed him, cut his hair and fingernails. I talked to him while doing all of this, even though his brain had likely stopped working. He was artificially ventilated and fed, had a tube in his bladder to drain the urine. The other metabolic waste products were disposed of by the nurses, meaning us.

During that day's doctors' round, the cardiologist, dermatologist, urologist etc., were congratulating each other on their successful treatment of this patient. I thought I was in the wrong film. The question mark in my head grew bigger and bigger. Until I began to wonder. Is this patient being perhaps being used as a spare parts store? Will he be gutted, and his organs that are still halfway okay sold to the highest bidder? It's what it felt like.

And what else? Body signals of failing health were silenced with symptom killers, feelings such as anger, sadness, despair, or excessive joy suppressed with pharmaceuticals. And if something got to someone's kidneys, they were given a tube in their bladder. People who no longer want to live are the first to refuse food. But they pay so well for care. We simply insert a tube and feed them artificially. It's scary, even cruel, what humans do to humans! Especially people whose lives have become mere infirmity.

That's why everyone should draw up an advanced directive in good time!

IDEALS

I was full of ideals when I started this apprenticeship. I wanted to do good, to help people. And then I realized that there were machinations in the healthcare system that I didn't agree with and was powerless to do anything about changing.

But there was one thing I could do. During a period of night-duty shifts, I painted a ward, creating visual treats to counteract the sorrow. It was a closed geriatric psychiatric ward. For years or decades, the people here had only ever seen these dreary walls. Now there was a certain excitement on the ward, curiosity. People came out of their shells and approached me: "What are you doing there, are you even allowed to do that?"

FOOL'S HANDS SMEAR TABLE AND WALLS

Even as a small child, tucked up in my little bed at nap time, I whiled away the time by painting on the walls through the bed's safety bars. Of course, I wasn't allowed to do that and my father scolded me at the time. But the fools on the ward obviously liked what I was doing. I used it to drive away my feeling of powerlessness in the face of this misery.

I had been well trained to ... Yes, to do what actually?

FEARS AND DREAMS

Speculation is mounting about a third world war. Doomsday scenarios ... it's unbearable! The war in the Gulf has already lasted two weeks. The sky over Kuwait was a cloud of black smoke, vast quantities of oil polluted the Persian Gulf. Pictures of seabirds completely covered in oil. Not to mention the thousands and thousands of people killed.

What kind of war was this? I was paralyzed, listening to reports on the radio being announced like song hits: "We're here for you live ..." I heard about demonstrations and didn't go. I rode my bike through a dome of smog in a city that had long since succumbed to traffic gridlock. The world was me. I felt with it and was on the verge of contracting a fatal disease. A mirror, so to speak, of the times around me. But before that, I wanted ... Oh, I wanted so much more, especially LIFE.

I found a new boyfriend, he moved in with me, and we both worked towards the common dream of exploring the world. This friend even cooked for me when I pulled a late shift! I had never known anything like that before. In any case, it really impressed me that someone was looking after me for once.

We found a third travel enthusiast and we three "Ossies" (people from former East "*Ost*" Germany) earnestly continued pursuing our goal. Locked up for umpteen years, we finally wanted to experience the wide, wide world.

I chose the first destination: Crete. And we set off. Relatively soon, it became clear that we had different ideas, goals, implementation methods, and tempos. One of us jetted straight to Kenya and blew his entire travel budget in three months. I fell in love with another guy and stayed on Crete for a while. Later, however, I kept running across the guy I'd started out with, first in Egypt, and then in India. After that, I never saw him again.

I'd entrusted my dog to my family and left my apartment to a couple I knew, who incidentally had one of my dog's puppies. My rent was paid automatically from my account via standing order. I'd made the practical arrangements. My subtenants were supposed to pay the rent into my account, but they didn't do that. Had I fallen in with the wrong friends again?

On my trip, I pretended to be poor and worked to get to know the country and its people better, which also helped me make friends. I avoided the tourist hotspots and spent at least three months in each country. I also spent three months on Crete, where I worked in a tavern. Then I went on by ship to Alexandria — all alone.

There I landed in a very foreign world. The first thing I noticed was that there seemed to only be men around. And they were holding hands! I now know that there are many countries where girls are separated from their male playmates, brothers, or friends as soon as they reach sexual maturity. They are locked up, separated. They are no longer allowed to see or be seen by boys until they are married off. They aren't allowed to have an opinion on this. The marriages are negotiated by the men.

What luck that I had to have grown up in East Germany! We were the best in the world when it came to equal rights, so we also had the highest divorce rate.

I then traveled to Dahab, to the Red Sea, learned the Arabic greetings, which I liked very much: "May the morning be full of light, smooth, like cream, sweet as honey!" Each person would say a phrase like this, then the other would reply and so it went back and forth for a while. Here, I worked in a beach café.

Then I went on to Israel. I found myself at the Dead Sea and soon had a job with a man called Israel. This was in the countryside near Eilat. Young people from all over the world worked here and there was dancing in the evenings. An Israeli woman asked me what I — a German — was doing there. She told me the Germans had murdered her grandfather. A long conversation ensued, at the end of which we were almost friends, or at least understood each other.

FREE BILLY

I remember picking melons with two men for the first time in my life. They were nagging me the whole time: Where are you, go faster, and so on. I was already doing what I could, ambitious as I was. I allowed myself to express my anger, tipped out the 15-kilo bucket and let the melons roll towards the guys. And then I let them have it, swearing and cursing all I wanted. I remember how good it made me feel and that I kept on swearing even when all three of us were laughing about it. It felt like a thunderstorm letting loose with a downpour after a long, oppressive sultriness.

And on we went to India. Here I didn't work, here I danced until I thought the ground would shake under my feet. I learned body surfing and saw fruit bats for the first time. I was drumming by a fire under a full moon when first one bat came, then more and more, and they circled over us. A wonderful experience, I still have the images in my head.

Wherever I went, I always found friends, like-minded people, soul sisters and brothers, seekers, finders. I noticed that no matter where I was, someone thought they remembered me or somehow confused me with someone else.

Goa and the surrounding area were by no means the end of this journey. I continued along the Ganges up into the Himalayas until I got too cold and the air too thin.

When I went looking for it in my diaries, I didn't find anything about this trip. These reports had ended up in a garbage can on Genter Strasse in Berlin, just like the other diaries I had written up to that point.

Back to the main story.

So after Goa, Arambol, and Anjuna, I followed the Ganges. This route was filled with people making pilgrimages to pay homage to their gods in one of the many temples. For example, there was an old man carrying a huge basket on his back. When he stopped at one of the many tea stalls, I was astonished to see his wizened wife climb out of the basket.

I arrived in Anapurna with a terrible earache. I found a doctor who gave me medication and arranged a room where I could recover. It was so nice to see that help was available when you needed it. This was also evident later. I had caught amoebic dysentery. For weeks I couldn't keep food or fluids down for long, had blood in my stool, was skin and bones, and felt miserable. I remember musing in my diary about being on the move like a river.

EVERYTHING FLOWS

And now an encounter of the third kind. A man approached me and said that I didn't look well and that he could help me. We sat down and smoked something together. Suddenly he said: "Shut up, I'm in a trance. I know you, you lived here once before, when you were a young man. Your name was Anamika Nadi, 'Nameless River.'" Then it got creepy. He started berating me about why I was always running away. He threw me completely off track with the following question: "Do you really think you don't have any friends?"

I was flummoxed! How could he read my mind, recognize me in this way, and affect me so deeply? I started crying and couldn't stop for ages. I wanted to get away from the hypocritically protective friends who were just using or coming onto me. I'd already experienced enough of that. But I just couldn't get rid of this guy. He stuck with me as I went on my way into the forest.

We passed a little house with a courtyard that was bustling with people. An Indian woman with dreadlocks down to her behind called us over. We weren't allowed to go any further because this was the realm of the animals. She was probably some kind of holy woman, I found out. She received gifts and was obviously very revered by her visitors. This woman whispered in my ear that I should stay with her. The man had nothing good in mind for me. Of course, I gladly accepted this invitation as I was at the end of my rope and feverish. When the visitors and the man had gone, the good woman offered me her own bed in the house that only had two beds. The other bed belonged to her acolyte, or servant, or whatever.

My new friend was definitely a healer. She made little marijuana pellets and gave them to me as she put it, to help clear up my stomach. She also gave me opium for the diarrhea and antipyretic tablets. Exhausted and relieved, I sank into the bed she'd offered me. I woke up at night because someone was taking advantage of my defenselessness and was grabbing at me. But I was so knocked out by the opium or whatever it was that I couldn't really defend myself. I didn't want to call for help either. The good woman had already done so much for me. But she was camped outside in the yard and heard that something bad was going on. She came in and shooed the creep away from me. The next morning she said that she would have liked to continue looking after me, but under the circumstances I'd have to go.

Despite all the freedom you can feel when traveling, every day the question, "Where will I sleep tonight?" must be answered.

I was on the road for 13 months — a year of unpaid leave plus normal vacation. For such a long period of time, I have very few memories of it. That's a shame, because every day was so different from the one before or the one after.

The tour had started on Crete and I returned there to come back to myself after flying so high. Besides, the time I'd planned to be away wasn't up yet and my apartment was still occupied by the subtenants.

A FATEFUL ENCOUNTER

I met HIM at the disco on Crete. I had never seen this boy/man before, that much was certain. Nevertheless, I shuddered. Oh God, no, I thought, I know him. And felt something like danger at the same time. But from the first moment we exchanged glances and connected, I was obsessed with him.

I pointed him out to my best friend and confided that I probably had a crush on him. She, who was much less shy than I was, dragged him to where we were sleeping on the beach. Once there, she really got down to business and quickly had him under her spell. So now I got to watch the two of them acting out their Romeo and Juliet story right under my nose.

Love is free, like a butterfly. Love is where it wants to be.

So, what was I supposed to do? I went swimming, what else?

The good thing about the sea is that when you are swimming in it, some of the problems of life on earth soon become insignificant. You become a small drop in the whole, no more, but also no less. Everything becomes light. Then you are one with everything and with everything as one.

TWO STEPS BACK

During my trip through India, I seriously considered for the first time that I might already have several lives behind me. That would explain why, in some encounters, you have such a certain feeling that you already know this person. And also why children experience such bad things, even though they have not yet been able to harm anyone in this life.

My beloved maternal grandfather said that the sum in life is a constant, what you give will be given to you, what you take will be taken from you. The much-discussed justice of balance. Perhaps in another life I'd been an executioner or a cutthroat and deserved every blow I got. But no, my child! Life is a boot camp, a training ground. Whomever the good Lord deems worthy, will be tested especially hard. He will only put as much on your cross as you are able to carry. Oh my goodness, is it love itself that tests us? There is a beautiful poem by Khalil Gibran. It's about what love does to you to make you as pure as white flour, to give you a pure heart: You are treated like the grain: broken, threshed, ground, and sifted. If suffering serves this lofty goal of becoming a better person, then I'm very thankful. It is important to let go of obstructive beliefs such as: I always do my best and in return, get a kick in the pants. Leave the victim role! It's hard to believe how quickly thoughts can manifest themselves. Everyone knows about self-fulling prophecies/predictions, right? It's all about learning. When you take on someone else's responsibility for, and burden of caring for themselves — and maybe go into debt yourself in the process — you're not being a good friend. Not to the other person, and not to your own self, either.

MOTIVES

I marched to a different drum, playing at love — Do I love you? Do you love me too? — instead of bonding. Various people suspected different things about me. My mother declared that I had a phobia of attachment to people, places, and jobs. According to the psychiatrist, I had bipolar disorder with psychotic episodes. An astrologer friend of mine was the first to tell me that I couldn't help it. I'm a Capricorn, ascendant Pisces, rational and irrational, a borderline rider between crazy and normal, the hereafter and this world. In the Chinese horoscope, I'm a fire horse and therefore sometimes almost impossible to reign in. I'm a left-hander trimmed to the right, which can also lead to irritation.

Nowadays, I'm so sensitive and empathetic that I need to spend lots of time by myself, especially after contact with other people. I easily lose myself in others.

And I still haven't managed to eradicate my childhood patterns, even though I'm a mature child of 56. I feel like a jigsaw puzzle that has come apart and I'm trying to rearrange myself. I am important, next-of-kin to myself. I can and must think of myself first. I can dare to be myself, because I'm like this, even though I'm like this, because I've always been like this. Because I can't be anything other than who I am.

I seek self-knowledge, self-awareness, respect for myself, as ME, SUPEREGO, IDEAL, and the imperfect being that learns through mistakes. I'm learning that I have the choice to react to the unexpected one way or the other: as a never-satisfied sacrificial lamb or as a self-responsible peaceful warrior.

I now know that certain tasks the ancestors couldn't solve are passed on to the next generation. We feel a guilt clinging to us that isn't ours, a hereditary guilt, possibly leading back directly to the original sin that affects our entire human race. We have destroyed paradise, elevated ourselves above the animals, gained power, and mismanaged it. And not for the good of ALL.

SYMPTOMS

It's good to stop and think about what is truly worth telling. I've experienced first-hand things that have destroyed my atheistic, rational view of the world. It's also about the great responsibility we have towards ourselves to keep our body, mind, and soul healthy. What burns on my soul, what I can grasp in my mind but can't express or communicate, manifests itself physically. I mentally take the symptoms' path.

As a child, I quite often showed symptoms of angina or mumps. This was to avoid having to go to kindergarten or because the relationship between my parents took away my ability to breathe. I wanted cancer because my brother had it and he got more attention after his death. I just missed him so much. I learned that people who die tragically get noticed.

And I imagined what it would be like one day if I died of cancer too. Will YOU regret not having noticed me at my grave? Later, when my breasts grew, I was embarrassed and tried to bind them because having them had suddenly changed the way boys behaved towards me. We had previously played together as if I was one of them. When I was 14, I got *muluscum contagiosum* — warts — all over my chest. I loved falling in love and making out. But I didn't just want my body to be desired and not my soul. So, the body became unsightly.

I also had this idea in my head: One day someone would cross my path and we'd realize we were meant for each other. And then they would find each other and live happily ever after. And if they haven't died, then they are still alive today and certainly as in love as they were on the first day. I fled when I was supposed to spread my legs. Or they left me because I wouldn't let them. Regardless, it was always very sad since I loved them. But I wanted more than just satisfying my animal instincts. I saw (and still see) myself as a soul wanting to be loved for my own sake. Not because my tits remind a partner of his mom's breasts, or because I do things that satisfy others.

What about me? As a left-hander, I scratch the crook of my right arm. So tenderly that I almost can't stand it any longer. Then I scratch it to get back to normal. Showing feelings isn't so easy and that's why there are and have been so many symptoms in my life. When I was unhappy, I'd get warts on the arm that I'd always scratched; when I was happy, the warts disappeared. When I was 23, I had 23 warts on my hands and feet. I couldn't do anything, I couldn't caress, I couldn't give or take. It couldn't go on like this, I couldn't go on. My feet hurt.

I'd had exactly the same thing as a child and an appointment was scheduled to have the warts surgically removed. I was terrified. My mother gave me the tip to run around our house three times during a full moon with rotten leaves in my shoe and then forget about the warts. I firmly believed in success if I tried it, and I did. It worked. The operation was canceled.

Then I took matters into my own hands, went to the park at night every time there was a full moon — my dog was happy — and took the opportunity to chase bunnies. I used a saying as a mantra to keep my head clear during my activities: "I'm going to leave it all behind, what makes me mad and sad and blind." Whether I was running or doing gymnastics, I always tried to overcome myself, to show myself that I was stronger than I thought. After a year, I was wart-free.

I now knew what self-healing powers I had inside me and how I could activate them: with imagination, full commitment, concentration, and action. It was about the materialization of thoughts. Perhaps this is where opinions differ. What is credible? Whatever works.

My worst relationship was with that Jekyll and Hyde type guy who could be so sweet and then terribly evil, regularly beat me up and then tearfully beg for my forgiveness. When it finally ended, I got cervical cancer. He was the first person I wanted to have a child with. (Of all people!) The child's name should be Felix, the lucky one. What an illusion. How could we have been parents when there was a war at home every three days? Why didn't I run away from this guy after the first fist to my eye? I was a slave and I can't quite understand how that could have happened to me. I'm usually so strong. Love blinded me.

He disassembled me, studied my diaries while I dutifully earned my living. And then interrogated me, Stasi style, about who I loved, how, when, and why, why it didn't last. I would love everyone anyway. Why should he believe now that our story was something special ... Whore!

Having talked himself into a rage, he locked the apartment from the inside, demonstratively put the key in the lock, pushed me into a corner, and beat me up at will. Once it was so bad that I wished I was dead, and I actually left my body and was gone. When I came to, I was kneeling on the mattress in the corner of the room and he was stunned. I had gone completely white and looked through him as if he wasn't there. This little escape saved my evening and raised questions. Was I able to leave my body in an emergency? Had I fainted? Then I would have collapsed limply. Another story that takes us to what is most important to me, to all the experiences that I might have classified as crazy if they hadn't happened to me.

It was during the war in Iraq. Would there be a world war or would all the harm we were doing to our environment ultimately kill us? It was the subject of environmental hygiene that really opened my eyes. How we humans are destroying the earth, depriving other creatures of their habitat, cutting down forests, making ourselves sick, and pulling the rug out from under our feet. I was not alone, we were all afraid and I was confronted with the prophecies of Nostradamus, according to which a great evil was imminent.

Engrossed in such bleak thoughts, I cycled to work at "Bonny's Ranch" at around 5.30 in the morning. It was still dark, the city was sleepy, the streets empty. With the clinic on my left, I had to cross the lanes. I looked carefully like always, found all the lanes deserted, and wanted to get going. Then a bang, a flight, and I was lying on the road, saw the car coming towards me and suddenly had the feeling that I was experiencing everything in slow motion. I wondered if I was ready yet, what else I wanted, and whether the car would stop before ... Was it the fear of death that made me lose track of time, or had I simply suffered a shock and therefore time seemed to pass differently for me? Would the car have stopped in time if time had passed normally?

It was only when the Mercedes driver got out and shouted at me, asking if I had eyes in my head. etc., that the clock started ticking again. I picked myself up, took what was left of my bike, and ran to work. It wasn't that far away anymore.

I was extremely lucky and got off lightly with a few scrapes and bruises. In any case, I'm grateful for the food for thought. My reaction: I signed up to do the night shift for a whole year and then wanted to take a year's unpaid leave to explore the wider world. I also decided to stop listening to the news. I wanted to be informed, yes, but I didn't want to have fear stirred into coffee every morning. It distracted me from finding my way and going my own way.

I wanted to bring more joy to my senses at the clinic and asked the team and bosses if I could beautify the dreary corridor. They allowed me to paint the whole ward during the night shifts if I could find the time. I was allowed to bring my dog with me. He was so loyal and easy to look after that I could let him run around freely in the park. He'd run back to me to make sure I was alright, and come when I whistled for him, no matter where we were.

I painted seven walls and accompanied 13 people to their deaths that year. Back then, it was Coxsackie viruses that carried off the old and the weak. I always opened the window when someone had crossed the threshold. I wasn't yet sure what to believe about the lives of the dead. There was something in the room that wanted to get out, and the faces of the deceased were usually peaceful.

I believed that I had communicated with my brother as a child (postmortem) because I had perceived it that way.

A book like this one behaves strangely. It writes itself. It isn't a chronologically correct biography because stories are constantly popping into my head that tempt me to follow their tracks.

My working days (and nights) at the hospital were over. I'd learned a lot and left a lasting impression ... colorful pictures of trees, meadows, and fields.

Last but not least, the following incredible story belongs to this time. I adored our ward doctor, and he found me interesting. We once played pool together and I was in danger of falling in love. Then I dreamt that I was at his house, talking to his wife. She asked me not to turn his head, because they were quite happy with each other and had children together. A good conversation, a pretty realistic dream, I still remember it today. The next time I saw the doc, I told him about it and described his wife to him and he asked where and when we had met.

Crazy, right? But it gets even better.

STRANGE

Before my big trip, I visited my grandma in Finsterwalde. She had survived her third stroke but was in a coma. My father visited her in hospital every day, but his mother was no longer conscious. Strangely enough, she was awake when I arrived. We wished each other a safe journey. She was a bit confused and told me to take some tissues from the cupboard, you never know. I left and she fell back into a coma.

After landing in Crete with my two friends, where I got stuck because I'd once more fallen in love with someone, I experienced a stormy night with my current lover with no end to the rain in sight. We were both so tired. The rain pattered on the tent roof from above, the storm seemed to chase back and forth between the walls of our haven. It had already rained so much that our tent was almost standing in a river. We leaned back-to-back against each other and tried to fall asleep. It was a state between sleeping and waking. Is the alpha wave the door out of space and time?

Suddenly it seemed to me as if I was floating under the ceiling of Grandma's living room, watching the black-clad relatives at the table. I immediately realized that Grandma must have died. And I was already back in the tent in the hot weather. The next day I called my mother.

"She's dead, isn't she?"

"How do you know that?"

"I dreamt it."

It's about such wondrous moments. Cracks in the matrix or time loops. There is something beyond space and time. The

Russians have carried out experiments in which they separated mother rabbits from their young with thousands of kilometers of space in between. They wired up the mother to measure her vital signs and brain waves and tortured the children far, far away from her. The measurement results proved that there are connections through which information and feelings can be exchanged, no matter how far apart the participants are. This applies to lovers as well as haters, and in general to beings that have a connection to each other.

With each of these experiences, I became more open to miracles and more cautious about simply accepting a preconceived truth.

Since then, I've always pondered what could actually be proven and checked first. I suspected that everything I'd learned so far could be completely different. Especially this thing with death. Next to love, it is the area of research that interests me the most.

LOVE STORIES AND THEIR EXCESSES

I was still living in Berlin with this man whom I was providing for, giving him a roof over his head, and thinking I loved him. I played the whore for him, and he regularly beat me up. He knew my diaries by heart, quoted from them verbatim when interrogating me, mocked me, hurt me so much inside and out. And I just couldn't get away from him.

He enjoyed it when I was too incapacitated to take care of myself. Then he took my money, bought extra nice glasses, an expensive bottle of something alcoholic, got me a porn movie. As if I would have enjoyed something like that. When I dared to say that I didn't like porn, he kicked me in the ribs with his cowboy boots and smashed the movie cassette on my nose so that it broke. Or he pushed me into bed and stabbed the mattress around me, cutting my panties off. Once he hit me in the face so hard that one of my eyes popped out and I pushed it back in. He grabbed my hair and pounded my head against the wall. I don't know how much of that crap is still repressed somewhere inside me. I've been told I have an elephant's memory. But I'm equally good at forgetting.

I allowed myself to be abused and yet I couldn't part from him. My mother had already threatened that if I went back to him, I could no longer hope for her help. So, I was beaten black and blue and fled from him to her.

Once she picked me up from my apartment. The tires on my

bike were punctured and we walked from Wedding to Hansaplatz. I wasn't sure if he was following us or if I was just imagining it. But he was indeed following us, as it turned out later. I would be safe in my mother's apartment, we thought. She went to work in the morning: "I can't find my key, but … you're here." I remember having a terrible nightmare that night: I'm on the run in a big house with spiral staircases, terrified of my pursuer, running for my life, escaping into a room and there, where I want to save myself, the one I'm on the run from is already there. I run out, faster, up the stairs, down the stairs again, into the next room, slam the door, and think I'm safe. And who is already sitting in the corner? Him, the aggressor. This is repeated a few more times until I realize that there is no escape.

And then I woke up.

I heard the door being opened with a key. My mother hadn't taken hers with her. Within seconds I knew: HE was there, the nightmare had become reality. He had followed us to my mother's apartment the night before and taken the key, which in our nervousness, we'd left sticking in the door lock outside. To make matters worse, he had pulled out a knife. What was I supposed to do? I promised him what he wanted to hear, that I would come back to him. I let him take out his anger on me. Still better than being stabbed.

After that episode, I promised I really wouldn't relapse. My wonderful family organized a rescue operation. I left Berlin for Swabia on a foggy night. I started a new life there, found an apartment and a new job. But there's no cure for love, however sick it may be. I lasted seven months in exile. Then I gave up everything again and arranged to see HIM in Berlin.

In the meantime, I'd been diagnosed with cancer and thought the most important thing was to listen to my heart. With everything that had happened between us, I couldn't be angry with him.

I thought I understood what motivated him and why he acted the way he did. And understanding inevitably leads to forgiveness.

But where was my compassion for myself? What good does it do the world if I understand a tortured being, forgive him but allow myself to be destroyed by his anger? Nothing! One step forward, two steps back.

Anyone who can follow me this far is very lucky. Because after sharing this bad memory, I'm remembering something funny from the time of the new beginning in exile.

I WAS HIDING MYSELF

I found a job as a nurse in Gailingen, near the Swiss border. I was at the end of my tether. I was starting over from scratch and had an empty apartment.

There were these bulky waste campaigns where you could completely furnish your home for free. I found two foam mattresses, among other things. But ... someone had probably farted on them or cried or worse. I had to wash those mattresses. Just imagine: I filled the bathtub, added dishwashing liquid from the kitchen, and soaked the first mattress. It foamed without end. Then I tried to wring this huge thing out and more and more foam piled up around me. I was in trouble and in great distress, but I was having lots of fun trying to tame these man-sized mattresses in any way I could. All by myself, I laughed my head off at the increasingly difficult task. The first laugh I'd had in years. As hard as it was, I finished the job. As the apartment had underfloor heating, the beasts dried out over time on the floor.

The Medieval regular canon, Thomas à Kempis, said that "Many people secretly seek only themselves in the things they do and don't know it," while German author Michael Ende spoke of the mirror in the mirror. Elsewhere I learned that we are attracted to a partner because they show us our unrealized possibilities. I had come across somebody who hated the world and life. Someone who could be nasty.

And yet I was dear Billy, who loved everyone and everything, no matter how terrible something seemed or how someone behaved. Understanding = forgiveness. I learned from this friend that it's okay to be angry sometimes. I was so ... far too friendly. Everyone was allowed to talk to me, even if I didn't want them to. I'd say something like: "Sorry, I'd rather be alone." But it didn't have any effect. Now I can say "Fuck off!" or give the evil eye, growl inwardly, so dangerous that some people stay away willingly.

The evil one was removed from my life, but I don't want to fail to thank him afterwards. Somehow, he softened something that seemed petrified inside me, perhaps the inner walls behind which I hid everything that had hurt me, that I was angry about, even furious about. That had now turned into cancer. Manifested anger and disappointment directed at myself. Further and definitely, I had terrible feelings of guilt that I'd talked myself into as a child: My brother had died because I didn't eat my food, didn't clean my room, wasn't good enough. Abused because I deserved it, divorced parents because I wasn't worthy of them rallying around me. That's what makes children tick. They feel responsible. They feel guilty. As a result, I did everything I could to be worthy, helpful, and good, to achieve something and get better and better at it to somehow earn praise, attention, appreciation, and even love. I swam, played music, did my best at school.

The cancer. I had a conization. A small tumor was cut out while I was healthy. But that wasn't the end of the story.

As in the kingdom of heaven, so on earth, as above, so below, as within, so without. Microcosm = macrocosm. Bad thoughts, sick soul, sick flesh. I've managed to get rid of warts in the meantime.

I'd have liked to have had an intact family, but with my talent for healthy, satisfying interpersonal relationships, I'm sticking to my childhood vow: "I'll never get married." I believe in the good core in everyone. And when someone does me wrong, I try to understand, and all anger or resentment dissolves and makes room for love again. But there's something rotten about it.

94

The first thing our instructor at the psychiatric clinic taught us was that it's best to eliminate sympathy and antipathy right away. All people must be treated equally well. Even murderers and rapists. This prompted me to read patient histories during night duty on the ward, to take an interest in why people had become the way they were, why they did what they did. And lo and behold, how could it be otherwise, they had been harmed in childhood. Yesterday's victims later became perpetrators. And so on and so forth. The violent father may have been at war before, had to kill on orders and could no longer cope. When he went to church with his family on Sundays and heard, "Thou shalt not kill" and "Peace, joy, all good, " he ran away and got drunk at a bar. Came home and absolutely had to hurt someone.

I'm not saying that I'm in favor of any form of violence, but I can understand that a person in a web of lies, hypocrisy, corruption, manipulation, and suppression of their own being, loses their temper and goes on a blind rampage. Everyone is a person with their own story. You can learn to heal your wounds. But first you have to be willing to look at them.

I'm trying to do that in the here and now.

AT THE TIME
OF THIS WRITING

My alarm clock has quit working. It's still ticking, but time has stopped. A crack in the matrix. Fun.

December 23, 2022: We are between the fourth and fifth waves of the Corona virus. Delta is now followed by Omicron, another mutation of the virus that spreads even more easily. People are unsettled, full of fear and opinions are divided. We are granted Christmas, but then we are thrown back upon ourselves. Whether vaccinated or not, no one is safe from infection, serious illness or death. We are told to stay at home and minimize contact. These are sad, existentially threatening times for many of us. School, studies, business, ordering food, and social contacts are only possible via computer. National borders are closed. An even more oppressive feeling of being locked up than I'd experienced in the GDR.

There are various theories about Corona's origin. It was a biological weapon, intended to weaken the Chinese as they were reaching for world power. Unfortunately, the attack got out of hand. It is also suspected that there is a powerful elite that wants to reduce humanity and make a lot of money on the side. Or that they want to inject us with tiny computer chips to have total control over the people. What is happening reminds me of the book "1984," which George Orwell wrote in 1948. In it, he describes a state system in which everyone has a large screen in their home from which they are monitored and receive orders.

"Big brother is watching you."

Mabe Mother Nature has simply had enough of disruptive humans. The terrible thing is that we can only guess. There is news for every conviction online. News and fake news. There are heated debates about which is the real truth.

I think, fortunately we're not at war, and I withdraw into myself.

It's April 5, 2022, day 41 of Putin's war against Ukraine. After the environmental disasters and Corona have caused fear and horror, we have a new blockbuster that will keep the ratings high and us humans in a state of shock. Quiet as a mouse. Fear all around us. I hate war. As a female — the sex that gives birth to life — as a mother who wants to protect her children, as a nurse who has healing in mind, and as someone who has accompanied the dying to their deaths, I simply can't understand why people go out and kill their own kind upon a madman's orders. Women, children, anyone, or thing they can get their hands on. Nowadays, completely different weapons are in use, capable of destroying entire blocks of houses and massacring their inhabitants. That makes me so angry. What can I do? Be peaceful with my loved ones, pay attention to the good. I don't know how many millennia these guys have been doing this crap. But one thing seems very clear to me: War is a man's business.

"Only when reason fails does violence set in."

It's time to find other ways. So far, we've been going round in vicious circles and world history is doing the same as me. History will keep repeating itself until we've learned something and move peacefully in our circles on a different level.

Mice just hump each other when they are aggressive, and then everything is fine again. I admit that in dangerous situations I also preferred the path of least resistance instead of letting myself be beaten up because of unsatisfied urges. What you won't do to stay alive!

February 9, 2023: I'm jumping through the ages like this on purpose. Of course, the war in Ukraine is still weighing on our minds and we are considering reintroducing compulsory military service in Germany. Many people are afraid that this war could degenerate into a world war. A few days ago, there was a terrible earthquake in Syria and Turkey. In Turkey alone, 150,000 people are now homeless. Where are all these people whose homes have been destroyed going to live?

Mad cow disease is also back on the agenda and large corporations are arguing about who will soon be able to get rich from the global water shortage. It is almost unbearable, and we are becoming more and more like displacement artists.

In 1990 and 1991 ... I was 23, 24 years old, we had just about digested the Chernobyl nuclear disaster. The big fear was that we would all get cancer. Nature was already in dire straits.

Do you still remember the tsunami? I know people who were there and lost their loved ones. And then the war in the Gulf. January 23, 1990: Iraq begins destroying Kuwaiti oil fields, Iraq attacks Israel with missiles ... Iraq threatens Turkey with war because Gulf Air Force planes take off and land at a Turkish airfield. Iraqi attack troops cross the Saudi Arabian border on a broad front and so on and so forth. Fear is always breathing down my neck.

Well, I'd just finished my professional training. I knew the madness, had learned that every action has its causes, reasons, and consequences, seen people die, washed corpses, and been permitted to experience all the areas of medicine practiced at the hospital.

It's scary and cruel what humans do to humans.

I was so full of ideals when I started this training. I wanted to do good, to help people, and I also recognized machinations in the healthcare system that I didn't understand but was powerless in the face of.

I was able to do something. I've already mentioned that I painted a ward while on a long stent of night duty, creating eye candy to combat depression. The fools liked what I did, and so I drove away my feeling of powerlessness in the face of this misery.

BLIND FOR LOVE

September 20, 1993: I've been very down for two days and it's probably because of a 10-page letter that HE wrote to me, in which he tries to prove to me with a thousand arguments that I love everyone anyway, and immediately afterwards that I can't love at all. That I was a lying piece of shit.

When you love, you believe the person you love. And when they say that you're not worth loving, you believe that too. I was happy that I at least received negative affection. Quite a lot of it.

I would like to point out that I don't want to play the victim. I accept all of life's challenges because this particular life has made me who I am today. It was hard training right from the start. Always with violence clothed in different costumes. At first, my father put me in mortal fear: "She'll learn to keep her head above water." Do you remember? My brother's death also gave me a huge shock. And not long afterwards, the fear of death again, locked under the comforter with a big hand over my mouth. The next incident was during swim training: Three boys I quite liked dunked me in the non-swimmer's pool. They were holding me on the bottom. I could see them. I was terrified and in danger and they had no mercy.

Why do I like the bad boys so much, or was I ...

When I was 17, I hitchhiked to Prague to meet up with seven friends at the main train station. There were two stations, though, and we missed each other. It was 1984 and there were no cell phones yet. Frustrating! On the way home, one of the lifts I'd gotten drove onto a forest path and was up to something else. I escaped by running away. In the middle of no man's land, I hitch-hiked right onto the highway and was lucky. A fat guy about 50 stopped and saved me, I thought. He invited me to eat at a rest stop and drove me to Berlin. He started boasting about how nice he was being and asking what was in it for him. Why don't you at least show me your tits or … Oh no! Not this again. I had my rucksack on my lap and luckily a traffic light had just turned red. I took the chance and jumped out of the car.

Violence was a recurring theme in my life. And it was called "love," imagine that. If you've experienced such a pseudo-love from an early age, that's probably the status you strive for and find again and again, even though it doesn't satisfy you. Because it has always been the case that I've had to satisfy the others. It doesn't matter what happens to me. I've already had the pleasure of working with a psychologist and a psychiatrist. But hey, who else knows me like I know myself? There's simply no one out there who can help me. I'm a helpless helper after all!

If someone asks me: "Can I do something for you?" I say: "No, please don't." I don't want to owe anyone anything, but on the other hand I throw help around.

There's something wrong. It stinks to high heaven. The secret addiction to being needed …

I read "Zweig's novellas" on the side. Stefan Zweig is a writer who illuminates the extremes of human motivation in a highly masterful, melodious form. He expresses all the terrible so beautifully that I sometimes think, who am I to believe that anyone could be interested in my own bumbling remarks. I'm not good enough anyway.

What nonsense! From day one, I've lived a life that was and is perhaps different from other people's lives. Not better or worse, but different.

Bookshop shelves overflow with biographies and memoires.

Who cares what I did and what I think? And yet I feel the need to clarify my story. I want to shed light on what I can so that I leave behind a clean slate one day. No original sins bequeathed to my children. No repeats of unhappy relationships.

One lover called me a self-centered narcissist. I found out that I'm very emphatic and always end up with narcissists because I'm exactly the right match. And in a test to find out whether I was exposed to narcissistic abuse as a child, I answered yes to 20 out of 20 questions. When you learn early on that you have to perform for attention ... and the reaction is something like: "Well, it's okay. You tried to do well, but it's just not good enough, could be better." Because this was the response to my longing for love as a child, I had to believe that I probably didn't deserve to be satisfied when it came to love.

Now I've known for years that you first have to love yourself in order to be able to love others. I'm quite confused at the moment. I'm wondering about everyone I love, my children, siblings, parents, friends: Do I love them or do I just revolve around them so that they love me? Grrrrrrr.

My mother says I've always been the good child. Yes, of course: quiet, modest, hard-working, always at everyone's beck and call.

"Good guys finish last." In German, we put this saying another way: "Nice people get bitten by dogs." In fact, last weekend, while visiting a bunch of rowdy guys, their dog bit me for the third time, although perhaps no one had ever petted it so nicely and extensively. Or, for comparison, the story of my first stint in a psychiatric ward, remember? Ten fingernails ripping through my skin in response to my gentle murmuring.

I'm good at listening, at paying attention, and as a nurse I've learned to read a person's mood from their facial expressions, gestures, complexion, smell, and so on. What they might need to feel better. I find that I can, and have been able to, be very nice, even kind, to the people who have been placed under my care.

You can't drink from an empty well. Or as a poem I know goes, "A jellyfish got washed upon the seashore, the sun parched it down to the last pore. Now, the jellyfish is no more."

That's roughly how I feel. A helpless helper. Someone who likes to give but has big problems with receiving. That's stupid and unfair. Someone else doesn't have the pleasure of being helpful to me. Confusing ... I can't get this sentence from my father out of my head: "The purpose of life is to be a useful member of society." When I became a nurse, he was finally satisfied, and when I had children, I was good. I don't know what he'd think about me no longer being employed in those two useful tasks ... antisocial couch potato bum, comes to mind. My battery is dead. I can understand myself, but somehow an expectation gnaws on me that doesn't belong to me, just I've made it mine. I'm still useful to my children when they need me, and I have a sympathetic ear for anyone who needs it. Just nowadays, my "in-box" for taking in outside info fills up quickly. This then leads to an interpersonal crisis, and I have to flee, preferably out into nature.

Helpless. I forget to eat and drink, although satisfying basic needs was the main issue with the patients and my children. I'm so wired, though, that I'll only allow myself, or be able to eat once I've finished all my tasks and everyone else is full.

Before my morning shift, I'd have coffee and a cigarette ... Take a deep breath ... Breakfast break: take your time to inhale the cigarette against the stress and have a strong coffee to get you going again. It's better not to have to pee so much during work hours anyway. In nursing, you quickly get the feeling that you're not good enough. You can't live up to your ideals of helping and being there for people ... Three to five minutes to administer medication. Hello and goodbye. Constant time pressure ...

When I think about it, I've spent my life swimming, running, and then also had to be quick at work and preferably as good as possible. As a mother of two children without the helping hands of their fathers, there was still enough to do after work: shop, cook, do the laundry, hang it up, put it away, and so on and so forth. And when I also had a boyfriend who wasn't a father and was competing with the children for the little bit of me that was left, things didn't look rosy. Fortunately, my father and his wife always helped out and gave me some breathing space. Thank you for that.

Writing a book like this, which is supposed to illuminate your whole life, is a wild adventure and one topic leads to another. Can anyone else follow me?

I've rushed through my life and when I go to the tavern during my vacation, I can't sit still for long. Unfinished work literally jumps out at me and I like to help clear away empty bottles and overfull ashtrays, align tables and chairs at right angles so that everything's in its place. They know me there and let me get on with it, and why not? It's helpful.

SHADOW WORK

I was the second child, second best in my class. There was at least one girl who was better at swimming. Even my best friends were more beautiful, more mature, more desirable. A shadow child is only noticed at second glance. And so it was that the guy I'd fallen in love with only found me after a good friend of mine had kicked him out of her house. I was just a stopgap solution. He called it love — I wanted to believe him.

It was now the fourth time that I had shared my one-bedroom apartment with a boyfriend. Today, I can't even imagine doing that again. I need space for myself, a place to retreat to. At the moment, I'm almost completely withdrawn because I feel like I'm a bit off my rocker.

What is certain is that I'm shocked at how submissive I was, and actually believed I wasn't worth anything. Basically, he was the one who didn't have his life under control. He was powerless and dependent on the favor of his landlady. He managed to project his powerlessness onto me through violent beatings, threats, and even death threats to family members and to me. On top of that, he had delusions of jealousy. Although he was the one who was always cheating, he suspected me.

I personally take offense that I didn't save myself after the first blow. Instead, I forgave him again and again because of the damage that had been done to him in his childhood. You can understand everything if you put yourself in the other person's shoes and investigate the causes. But to forgive? My goodness! I started forgiving very early on in life. If someone smacks you in the face, just turn the other cheek. That's how I was ... anything but saintly, more like constantly hurt. He hated the world, people — and probably himself too. I'm still unshakeable in my belief in the good in each of us. IN SPITE OF EVERYTHING. First, the bottom line: I've learned to be bad, and he may have gotten a little nicer. Thank you. It was just training. Balancing.

On October 1, 1993, I fled Berlin with the help of my family. I first went to live with my aunt, my mother's sister, who was a Capricorn like me. Besides giving me shelter and attention, she also gave me this saying: "Everything can always get better." Thank you for that, my dear.

For seven months I tried to get away, built a new life for myself, found a great job in Gailingen. I looked after a group of 11 children who had previously all been in comas for months. It was shared housing, and I basically took over the mother's job. I woke the children in the morning, helped them wash and dress, made breakfast and beds, and took the children to their respective therapies. Went to the shared apartment, cooked lunch, picked everyone up again, and gathered them around the table. Shall I tell you how I won them over? With a loud burp. My mother used to burp at the table sometimes for fun and then look at me reproachfully. "Annette!" It wasn't me, but I still found this projection funny. In the meantime, my daughter has become the unabashed burper. The things you pass on in life.

One step forward, two steps back. How I squirm and would like to skip over the things that torment me. So I only ever write down fragments of the stories, just as much as I want to remember.

October 2, 1993: The only person I spoke to on my journey from Berlin to Tuttlingen was a young woman who had been evacuated from Berlin by her parents. And for the same cool reason, to free her from the clutches of her boyfriend, who would otherwise have destroyed her. Coincidence? More like a mirror within a mirror.

October 3, 1993: I want to remember so that I can forget. You destroyed everything that was dear to me, plants, pictures, instruments, diaries. You locked me up, tortured me with interrogations, your hatred. You beat me — more and more, more and more brutally, again and again, you were jealous of all the people who had ever played a role in my life. Idiot me. Why did I allow you to read my diaries? You studied my past, ravaged it and I hoped for understanding. Our love never had a chance to blossom, so suspiciously guarded and constantly doubted.

Everything I've worked for over the years is gone. My apartment, my independence, my job, my freedom and fearlessness, my belief in the power of love, my hope for us.

For fear of losing me (as a lover, breadwinner, landlord), you scared me so much that I left Berlin in a hurry. There's no going back, all the bridges have been broken. Here I am now, in the middle of nowhere with my backpack and bike. A wreck, broken, at the end of my rope, dependent on my relatives' help, and that after having stood on my own two feet for eight years. Start all over again. Don't turn around! Sometimes my insane love confuses my mind, I have crying fits, I want to go back to you and die by your hand rather than live without you, I long for your good side, which captured me so much that I always forgave you for what you did to me.

I don't want to forget it or where it has taken me. My pride is gone and so is my sense of what is allowed and what is not. No one should ever hit me. I don't know of any reason that would justify such a thing. I detest violence and yet I accepted it from you again and again, I'm partly to blame for what happened.

In the end, I was no longer in control of myself. As soon as you came near me, I was ready to get involved with you again, with you and your dreams for us. We wanted to love each other, set off into the world on our bikes, have children one day, a house by the sea, grow old together, be good friends, bite the dust together. Dreams! We loved each other too, we love each other ... BUT ... I wanted to voluntarily go to the nuthouse or a shelter. That's what my first steps away from you looked like. I gave up my life, I couldn't protect myself from you and myself, from this crazy force that pulls me towards you. It's still pulling and I'm struggling, and it hurts. I know we both want each other. The dilemma would repeat itself. Never in my life has anything or anyone scared me as much as you. (That's not true. I'd just repressed a lot of things, split them off.) And yet I love you, I miss you, I long for you, I wish that you would fall on your feet, finally become free, no longer want to make yourself dependent, be able and willing to take care of yourself — out of your own strength; because only then, when you no longer need anyone, can you really love ... voluntarily. And I hope — whether that's realistic or not — that I'll meet you again then.

April 11, 2022: Up to then, I'd repressed all the other acts of violence my loved ones had given me.

My father once called me a POSITIVE POINT IN A NEGA-TIVE WORLD. The nicest compliment I've ever received. BUT yesterday I found this quote from C. G. Jung: "Every psychological extreme secretly contains its opposite or is otherwise closely related to it. There is no sacred custom that does not eventually turn into its opposite. The best is most threatened by diabolical distortion, because it has suppressed the worst most of all. No one stands outside the black collective shadow."

Whether the following is also from Jung or from another clever mind, I don't know, but I love this saying: "Evil is the good, tormented by its longing for itself." The dark parts that I suppress within myself come at me from the outside. So, it isn't the case that I had burdened myself with guilt in a past life and was struck for the sake of balancing things out. No, the good child had avoided being bad sometimes. Just don't stand out and if you do, then by performing at your peak.

Before I fled Berlin, I left a 25-page letter together with Robin Norwood's book, "When Men Learn to Love" outside my apartment door, anxious not to be caught by HIM. As soon as I was left alone in my aunt's apartment, I called my old number just to hear his voice. I didn't say a word, but my heart plummeted when he picked up.

October 14, 1993: One of your blows to my eyes made a hole in my retina. It was repaired with a laser to prevent it from getting bigger and the retina from detaching, which would have led to blindness.

And despite everything, I love you, crazy, isn't it? Blind with ... Love. Why am I like this, that I have to leave people who really love me, push them away and fight for those I can't reach? I fight for the impossible and cling to it until I give up on myself. Why do I love the most those who give me the least in return, who treat me the worst, who fleece me like an Easter lamb? Why do I only ever want to give and not take? Being able to take also means admitting that you are weak and need others.

It dawned on me at an early age that I could do everything on my own. I was alone, especially when it came to emotions. I had to deal with my grief by myself. In my weakness, I looked for weaker people (animals) to be strong for them.

October 17, 1993: Disappointment, the end of deception, disenchantment, awakening, bitter medicine swallowed in the name of freedom so as not to die from the spell.

"You have to go too far to see how far you can go." Thank you, Heinrich Böll. And thanks also to Elias Canetti for this quote:

"There is a dangerous power in mistrust: it leads one to believe that one can think alone, judge alone, decide alone. It tempts you to believe that you are alone. It forces the others who belong to you to humiliate themselves and present themselves as if they had sinned. It erases the boundaries between what really happened and what is possible and makes the suspects guilty in all cases."

What I constantly talk about to others is my problem: love, friendship, to be and to let be, freedom, taking my life into my own hands, fulfilling my dreams myself, not relying on others because I only know what I want myself.

It can easily happen that I'll make mistakes along the way and get lost in the process and journey of finding myself.

October 1993: Suppression ... I know pressure from swim training. I have learned to fight against myself, against my limits, have tried to surpass myself, still do it at the risk of my life. Climbing mountains that scare me, swimming out into the sea — further than ever before, always pushing the boundaries of what is possible.

I have let you, my love, cross many boundaries. I want to know if there is a chance that one day I will be so strong that you won't be able to make me small. Or whether you want to become strong so that you no longer punish anyone else for your weakness. The evil you assumed about me was that I would leave you one day. I withstood all your attacks so that you would realize that I would stay with you. It almost killed me. And then indeed, you'd have been proven right. I'd be gone, have left you.

I believed your love.

April 11, 2022: It upsets me. This not being able to let go. It upsets me precisely because 29 years later I'm in a similar boat again. I can't get away from this kind-hearted guy who unfortunately gets on my last nerve and is obviously not good for me. He makes me feel like a mother who is with a child who demands all her attention. When I'm with him, I feel invisible, unheard, misunderstood.

Please, tell me how I can eradicate this behavioral pattern. Time and time again I come across people who love to get worked up about the wickedness of the world. They talk themselves into a frenzy of hate, search for people to blame and want to slaughter them. At the same time, their own lives are slipping out of their hands. And when I try to point them to the here and now, the beauty of the world, my own responsibility, my life slips out of my hands again. Correction: Slipped out of my hand, I should write, because I will leave all these unhealthy behavior patterns behind me!

November 11, 1993: What's crazy about me is that I have the urge to convince the whole world that I'm lovable. I will learn to live with the fact that there is at least one person who hates my guts. I will learn that the most important thing is to look after myself, to fight for myself and not against myself.

I went to the swimming pool and worked out my aggressive impulses. A man of about 60 approached me about my tattoo, the bird of paradise, and showed me his self-made one: an island. He told me that as a young man he had dreamed of living and working on an island with a few nice people, sharing the harvest. It didn't work out. Unfortunately, there are people who grasp power, oppress others, and live at their expense. How right he is. I have one great hope, and that hope is me. I would have given myself to you, that wasn't the problem. But I wanted to grow with you and not die because of you.

November 12, 1993: I must go to the hospital, my PAP smear wasn't okay, my uterus needs to be tweaked. That's no coincidence either. All physical ailments have their origin in the mind or soul. As soon as the danger is averted on the outside, it comes crawling out of me. Tired of life? Or do I want to see them all weeping and repenting at my grave?

I wanted a child with HIM ... of all people! What a self-delusion! I countered the sick reality with an ideal that could only destroy me. My uterus, my body, took care on my behalf that I didn't conceive a child. Thank you.

You don't deserve that I still waste loving thoughts on you, that I mainly see the good in you, that I pity your poor sick soul. At a certain age, you can and must decide whether to use your energy for good, growth, and prosperity or for violence, destruction, and vampirism. Get out of my dreams, thoughts, and feelings. Go, go, go, I never want to see you again!

You wondered why I only seem to have male acquaintances. I feel like I have more in common with the male sex.

And yet, here you are, still in my head and on it. My first gray hair bears your name. I have a great longing. I long for you so much. I lost myself in you and it was like you erased me. I'm looking forward to my laughter, my ideas, my imagination.

BILLY, with whiskers, a deep voice, and that special feeling for feminine men. I know that people have both sides to them: the feminine and the masculine. But in a world where women are still oppressed, I prefer to show that a woman is also man enough.

How lucky I am to be such good friends with nature. It gives me a home, wherever I am. I was by the river in the storm and rain, looked at stones and got involved in a chat with swans.

"Come, I'll show you how great my love is and kill us both," sing the Toten Hosen. In "Narcissus and Goldmund," Hermann Hesse wrote, "... not only everything fair was in the mother, not only sweet blue love's gaze, charming, happy smile, tasting consolation; in her, somewhere under graceful covers, was also everything terrible and dark, all greed, all fear, all sin, all misery, all birth, all having to die ..."

Yes, women, mothers, saints, whores, witches. Obscure objects of desire, so misunderstood by men and certainly much feared.

Every man was once dependent on his mother, at her mercy. Even if they are later driven to follow the call of nature to produce offspring, they are dependent on the favor of the female. Humans are like animals in this way. We are animals. We just hide behind a different name.

This job with the children in need is a good place for me to learn kindness, boundaries, assertiveness, and so on. I can let my maternal instincts run wild here.

But right, it's all about helping people to help themselves, and it would be bad if I were to behave as if I'm the one needing help like in the past — very bad!

November 16, 1993: There was a time when I was quite sure that I didn't want children because I saw that this world was coming to an end. I had learned which achievements of civilization lead to which diseases. I studied Nostradamus, followed the news, and noticed how wars and catastrophes were repeating themselves at ever shorter intervals. Watching which animal species are dying out because industry is displacing nature. I know how the human population is growing exponentially, how knowledge is replacing belief in and wisdom about the connections. Specialists are turning into idiots because they don't communicate and thus lose sight of the big picture.

In the mental hospital, I found the failures of human interaction, a system with outsiders, the rejects. And now — a carcinoma has been removed from an otherwise healthy me — I live with the thought of what happens when I only have a short time left.

In view of the misery around us, it is so important not to give up hope. I'm not blind! In a certain sense pessimistic because I'm a realist, but also an optimist and fighter within the scope of the remaining possibilities.

April 11, 2022, 7.08 p.m.: I've just grabbed something to eat, breakfast so to speak. There are still demonstrations here on

Mondays and I asked a couple what they were still protesting against and they said, "Well, they still want us to get vaccinated." Alfa, beta, gamma, delta, omicron ... In my opinion, the coronavirus has now become so weak that you are as unhealthy after an infection with it as you would be with a flu-like infection. It won't be long before we let our own immune system fight it, and then we will certainly be better protected than by a vaccine that in my view doesn't really help, not against infection, not against illness, and not against death.

I decided to get vaccinated for several reasons. If it helped, I wanted to benefit from it, too. I also wanted to be allowed to travel. Additionally, and in the name of freedom, I used some other methods to protect myself from diseases. But it's probably too late now for the politicians we elected to push through decisions just to show consistency and not lose face. When Mr. Spahn, Germany's former health minister during the pandemic was infected with Covid himself, I wrote him a card and recommended colloidal silver against bacteria, viruses, and fungi. I don't know whether my message got through to him. But isn't it nice when ordinary citizens follow the discourse and contribute their own thoughts and ideas?

A joke from the time of the fall of communism in East Germany went: "We are *das Volk* (the people) and my name is Volker."

For 41 years now, my practice has been to be in a quiet room or space and then journal away, writing down everything that bothers, touches, or moves me, even though I felt nobody was interested in my opinion anyway. And now I feel a certain elation. If I share my experiences, maybe someone will recognize themselves in them. Maybe I can offer solutions, help.

I don't know what I would have done if I hadn't had books. It seems like I was always running across the exact story or tale I needed to help me move forward on my path. I started with fairy tales by the Brothers Grimm. Then my father read Karl May and Wilhelm Busch to me. Soon I was reading on my own. The Prometheus story, Hesse, Böll, Fried, Fromm, Zweig, Krishnamurti, Gibran, Canetti, Coelho ... It's impossible to list everything. I found answers to many questions. But it was up to me to put all the wisdom I read into practice. Every insight was followed by a "... what still needs manifesting is ..."

My daughter asked me if she could have my books after I've passed on. That made me very happy. For the time being, though, I'm reading them myself and keeping my eyes out for useful bits that can inform my remaining life. Maybe I can help myself in the process.

I'm reminded of the three sieves Socrates' said should be used as filters: Before you speak, you should ask yourself if what you plan to communicate is true, important, and good. I've already written a lot of things that weren't good. But before I can eradicate mistakes, I first must recognize and name them. That's important to me. A dream: Two children, one keeps stumbling because it has a different gait. But because they are holding hands, they both fall and bump their heads. It's better to walk free. Everyone has their own timing and must have their own experiences and make their own mistakes, because mistakes make you wise. So, one is not enough. I'm a walking collection of quotations. Their creators may forgive me. I don't want to adorn myself with other people's feathers. Everything has probably already been thought through and described anyway. But not yet by me. And that is why I'll simply keep writing in the way the words come out through my hands.

Paper is patient and my little machine also has time.

Working your way through the swamp isn't easy and I've almost been forgetting to even eat. So, I've taken a break from writing for the past two days and focused on the here and now. I've created

117

a little tomato bed on the windowsill, cleaned the hallway, and planted all the various cuttings that had already taken root in a jar of water in good soil. Positive acts to counter the bad feelings. Good soil for strong roots. A clean way out ... from the secret addiction of being needed.

Again and again, I've sought or found the opportunity to love selflessly, for the sake of my parents, for the sake of my patients, for the sake of my lovers, for the sake of my children ... while putting myself on hold. I don't even know what I want. To be a useful member of the community ...?!? I want to be heard. Especially heard by my own self ... I've always loved myself, but I put other people's well-being ahead of my own. First, I take care of the dog, cat, mouse, child, and birds, clear away the garbage, and only when everything is done, all the homework so to say, do I look for the right moment, a hiding place that's quiet and peaceful and private. Then, I feed myself.

As if self-care is a bad thing.

HOMEWORK

... give up! I've always done everything for others, for society. And why do I feel so drained now? Because I did so much more for others and forgot myself in the process. And because I can't accept anything. Do I want help? No, thanks and please don't! I've always done everything on my own. I know best how I want it to be. Can I be helped at all?

I'm a perfectionist and I want things to be the way I've imagined they should be. It would be lovely if I did my part, you did yours, and then we could rest against each other or stir each other up and then relax again.

It's April 13, 2022, and I'm alone, but boredom and loneliness are strangers to me. My spirit is speaking and I'm talking to myself as if I were in a group therapy session. Perhaps I'm a split personality, alone in such a motley group.

I've now read through 3 of my 48 journals, skimming at times as I'd probably rather look ahead, distract myself. But it seems necessary to me that I settle accounts with the past.

Every being has its right to exist and is good enough simply because it is. Me too ... and YOU! What do I want? To find out who and where I am and what my next ... ha-ha ... homework assignment is. I feel trapped in a vicious circle. And I'm certainly not the only one. Thanks to Corona and the resulting "solitary confinement," many people have just realized that it all depends on themselves. There have never been so many memoires, autobiographies in the bookshops.

I think that's a good sign. We've all been tossed into a state of self-reliance and are slowly realizing that everyone has to help themselves first. Love yourself first ... and then others.

That, I believe, is the change we can make: putting one's own self first. Love yourself as you love your neighbor ... But how? First pay attention to yourself and then it can wander outwards. I can feed myself first. Every animal knows that. But as a human, I've learned something that is bad for me. There were times when there was nothing left of my food when I'd finally got my homework all done.

In 1991/92, war was on my mind, the ongoing "Gulf War" and all the wars that people were waging. The environment that was being destroyed more and more. I felt sad and powerless.

Then a war broke out in my one-room apartment. With the person I was closest to: me. The prospect of a possible early end to my young life awakened my self-preservation instinct, my fighting spirit. Here, with just me, myself, and I, there was strength. I wasn't powerless. If I'd managed to talk myself into cancer, I would be able to talk myself out of it. Just like the warts on my hands and feet that I'd successfully talked myself out of. Body, mind, and soul, an inextricably interwoven system.

All beings are just as intrinsically intertwined, including individuals, couples, families, village communities, cities, states, and the entire world population. Everything is interconnected with everything else. Like the trees with mushrooms in the forest or all of us now on the WWW, the global Internet.

I've been talking for ages now about the need to start a revolution within our own selves which can then improve conditions around the world from the inside out. And now I must admit that this revolution is a lifelong process. It isn't enough to just talk about theoretical solutions and leave it at that. Ingrained behaviors are difficult to discard. And there may be relapses. But you shouldn't let this discourage you. At some point, the pressure of suffering will be great enough. You realize how urgently a change for the better is needed and finally take decisive action. Being diagnosed with cancer was a challenge for me. My dream realization program was far from finished.

15.04.2022: Good Friday, Putin has been sending his troops against Ukraine for 70 days and people are remembering Jesus, who supposedly bears the sins of humanity on his cross. Thanks, man, but that doesn't work, I've already tried it. You can't carry your brother's cross.

I wonder what Mr. Putin thinks? It's mindboggling what drives people to unleash all-out murder again and again.

In a film I saw today, a woman had an idea: Unite all mothers of the world to put an end to this madness once and for all.

"No, I won't give up my sons," is a good song by Reinhard Mey on the subject.

And by the way, going back to the war that is still raging inside me: I've prescribed myself solitary confinement and can't get out of it. My heart and my mind don't see eye to eye. What I have just conjured up from the past can be found right here and now. A magical, not magically beautiful attraction between two people who can't let go of each other. He can't understand that my battery died when he was at my side. No one here can understand me ... But didn't Germany's famous comic, Otto, already say that?

I'm simply good at understanding and empathizing with others.

Learning is learning. It seems to me that I often come across people who want everything to revolve around them. Am I like that too? Mirror in the mirror? I write and it's all about me. Children, patients, lovers only want me to satisfy their own basic needs. Or: I only want to satisfy others' basic needs and thereby make them dependent on me. Do I not even know what love is? Abysses open up ... That can't be. I love with every fiber of my

121

being ... For example, stones, stars, the sea, and so much more, simply everything, even if it's the shadiest end of the beam of light.

Do I love myself, too? That sounds like an anxious question from deep inside of me. Of course, why not? I don't know. I have very high expectations of myself and feel inadequate right now. I'm trying to give myself what I would have liked from others in the past ... attention. But seeing so many mistakes is only fun up to a certain point.

Shortly after my father's death, I started my first book for the world. It felt like it was his last post-mortem homework assignment for me. He died in July 2020 and the book was finished on December 31, 2020 — a little Bible for sensitive people. I gave it to a friend to read and we talked about it yesterday. I was delighted that she'd finished it so quickly and when she told me how interesting she found it and how much she'd like to know what happens next, it almost made my skin crawl. Her advice was to give it to my mother, to whisper it into God's ear!

But my mother doesn't want to know about it, isn't interested or would rather have peace of mind. She sends me biographies about other people. I admit my disappointment, mixed with understanding: Her poor heart is already stumbling anyway. Now this research trip is about why I make my love life so difficult. Her verdict early on was: "You always choose the wrong boyfriends."

And indeed, for a while it looked as if the story wasn't getting better from boyfriend to boyfriend, but rather worse and worse.

November 18, 1993: I just like to do battle. Preferably for the unattainable. Because as long as I don't achieve what I'm fighting for, I'm alive, I'm free.

I still feel torn, confused, mixed up — crazy, but no matter, I like myself.

April 17, 2022: Yes, exactly! It must be unattainable, love, just like back in kindergarten. Father? Mother? It's almost unbelievable that a person as mature as I am, is still stirring up this old shit from my childhood. Once again: I'm not trying to elicit pity or play Billy the victim. There were other (worse) kinds of suffering. And I see life as a boot camp: That which doesn't kill us makes us stronger and our hearts more supple.

1993: I remember that I was once invited to a family dinner at HIS house. He sat between his mother and me and held hands with her. That made me feel very strange. He always had her photo with him right along with his ID documents. I wished it had been a picture of a dog. I was cut off from my parents very early on.

"The mind is capable of doing more when it returns frequently to a difficult problem than when it dwells on it without interruption," said Harriet Taylor Mill.

The doctors are going to have to cut me open. Cancer or not, that is now the question. Either way, whether the world ends at some point, or I really do have cancer, it doesn't matter! I will live. I want to! I don't have time to lie around in hospital. There's a lot to do. I'm getting an own apartment on December 1st, 1993, and I don't want to rest until I've found my peace again and got rid of the shadows of the past.

The other day, someone stole a valve from my front wheel, and I thought HE really had the power to find me anywhere. When a phone rings somewhere, I feel a shock in my limbs. Fear has been my companion for a long time, but it's slowly getting better. That should've been a lesson to me, but my foolish heart still hopes for a 180-degree turnaround on his part and a happy ending with him. I'm blown away ... Simultaneously fear, horror, and an insatiable longing for the one who got me into this mess.

Can you understand that? If you don't want to hear, you must feel ... unknown. I failed in my knowledge of human nature, didn't listen to my inner voice ... the big NO at first sight. And ... what business is it of his, my diaries, love stories from other times?

I didn't realize that he was suffering from a mania of jealous delusions.

Inner voice? Ha-ha! My inner voice speaks with two tongues. Just as I can write left and righthanded at the same time, left-handed in mirror writing and right-handed correctly, I think in two different directions at the same time... back and forth. Emotion and reason at odds.

I want freedom and security. I'm simultaneously in this world and in the other world, realistically rational and at the same time a spy who reads the truth between the lines and sees signs that only I understand. Is it any wonder that I'd find someone who loves and hates me at the same time? And you, my beloved enemy, were also split between the urge to keep me and the urge to get rid of me. The two of us a powerful team that fit like a glove. Hate and love ... and because I can't hate you, I feel powerlessness and love.

In "Narcissus and Goldmund" by Hermann Hesse, I found:

"You look so cheerful, but inside your eyes there is no cheerfulness, there is nothing but sadness; as if your eyes knew that there is no happiness, and that everything beautiful and beloved will not stay with us for long. You have the most beautiful and saddest eyes, probably because you are homeless."

I've often been told I'm always in a good mood. But I'm more of a melancholic. I know how fleeting happiness is. Everything created can also be destroyed again. We're born to die.

Another sentence from Hesse: "It does not matter what and how much a person reads, the coincidence of what is read is important." Converted: It doesn't matter who and how many a person loves; the coincidence of the beloved is important. We can't choose who we fall in love with. It's a matter of resonance, of wavelength, of attraction. We should learn from and with each other. Aleister Crowley said it was a physical law that we find exactly the right person in the right place at the right time.

And now Hesse once again: "Love is not there to make us happy, it is there to train the heart's capacity for suffering." And that's why I thank life for EVERYTHING. Now I'm alone, but one with everything.

Is it true that the price of freedom is loneliness? And if so. Everything I need is within me. Your violence is just a silent cry for love, to be lifted up, to belong, and be recognized. If I allow violence against my person, I'm the one doing it to myself.

April 17, 2022: Let's remind ourselves once again: life is a boot camp. Or like this: Once upon a time, there were archangels who could do almost anything. They just couldn't feel. So, they removed their wings. Or invented humans, who now had a wide variety of experiences and were therefore supposed to feel the whole range of emotions from sorrow to joy, hate to love, helplessness to happiness, and so on and so forth. I agree with C. G. Jung's view of the collective unconscious, which, like every child, wants to learn and grow.

I think of my body as something like a car for my soul. If the car breaks down, I'll find myself a new one, if that's what I want. I'm not so sure about that yet. Did I mention that I was briefly dead? Dead, but not dead after all. It was the most beautiful feeling of being ALL ONE that I've ever experienced. When I realized that I was meant to live again, I wasn't thrilled at first, because living definitely means suffering. That's simply the best way to learn.

1993: Found a newspaper article: "How do I saw my child apart?" Children of divorce feel torn between anger at and love for their parents. But they can't process their emotions because they don't yet understand that people are sometimes good and sometimes bad. The danger exists that a feeling of guilt will accompany them into adulthood. It's possible that a child will say bye-bye to both parents and escape into a dream world populated only by good people. This results in a naive knowledge of human nature and being powerless in conflict situations. They see no way out and no way to let the evil out for fear of being abandoned."

My parents passed the buck to each other, and I said goodbye to both of them. When my mother had another child, I was 15 at the time, I took on the father's role. Later, I was the strong partner of the weak.

And what about abandonment? Do I leave my partners out of fear of being abandoned? Like with my brother, the teddy bear, my parents, my first great love ... ? What happened to the batterer? Why didn't I kick him out after the first assault? Maybe because I thought I'd finally figured it out. That GOOD and EVIL dwell in one person, that perhaps the greatest happiness can only be experienced in connection with the greatest suffering?

In India, in the place called Kali Mata (Mother Nature), the thought occurred to me that the meaning of life is the very simple one of coming together and having a child. The simple thing that is so difficult to do. I wanted to remain free — but not to climb into bed with all and sundry.

Free to be myself, because I had learned that as a "female" in a couple, I put on a jacket that didn't fit me. Didn't want to be the private whore, didn't want to be the mom, didn't want to be the dad. Above all, I didn't want to be seen as property. I'm looking for a brotherly friend.

"And may your love grow into strength that radiates to others," is a nice wish or blessing for people in love.

You shouldn't be so selfishly closed off to the other person when you love each other. Maybe all these experiences are just tests of fire, low blows, so that I can really appreciate the highs in life. Or maturity tests to see whether I accept everything that life offers: love and suffering, day and night, creation and destruction, birth and death. EVERYTHING is part of it. All of this is life.

November 26, 1993: A nightmare. Oh, dark black soul. In a big house I was on the run from him, and he had become a monster. He pulled out a knife and half-laughing, half-desperate, ordered me to hug him. Then he took his clothes off too, phew! In front of me stood a creature, bloated and full of thick pus-filled bumps with large breasts and an overlong cock. He would have gone mad because of me, he cried, and I hugged him, feeling nothing. Now he had become one man and one woman, and I should look at what had come out of it. It was all my fault. GUILT ... just a dream!

Take courage, Billy, my dear!

Well, Annettchen, can't you remember that you once set out to learn to be afraid? Your life was supposed to be an adventure. Thank you, I've had enough of fear, but it was definitely an adventure. I've realized that fear is in me, but so is love.

December 1, 1993: The ribs have knitted, the broken nose has healed, the retina has reattached, only the right index finger is still damaged and hurts when I write: the touch-your-own-nose finger. Is it only what I allow to happen to me? Nonsense.

I've chained myself to two lucky charms: my mother's divorce ring and my paternal grandmother's engagement present from her husband-to-be. A ruby set in gold to remind me that I still have the chance to have a good family life. Unlike the people who gave me these things. Grandma didn't make it. The war was to blame. Mother didn't, the death of a child intervened. So, it's my job to make the story better.

It's worked well so far, ha-ha.

I know that people can experience things from their own strength that they never even dared to dream of. That's where I want to go and never lose control of myself, never harm others. I want to be good, to live well.

I feel just like a stranger in a foreign country, will I ever find anyone who understands me? There is such a loneliness — in the sense that although there are people around me who I know, who also tell me that they like me, they only understand me in the way they want to or can. Being alone in the middle of nature, far away from civilization is easier. Outdoors, I'm one with the universe. Although, being alone in the big city isn't that difficult. All my senses are distracted, everything just scratches the surface: my car, my house, my hair, my fingernails, cosmetics, soccer, TV series, and these people who talk about others behind their backs.

I'm more concerned with the meaning of life and death and the rich world of emotions. I believe in Great Forces and want to see who wins: Good or Evil, Life or Death. Or is the battle only fought when the "OR" falls away, when everything IS ONE again?

Cervical cancer ... the physical manifestation of this dilemma: I love longing. I'm damn scared of giving myself completely, of reaching the goal of longing, of love. I go through heaven and hell, put myself in danger so I can be happy to have survived afterwards. Why am I doing this? A joke: Tell me, why do you always bang your head against the wall? Because it's such a relief when it stops hurting.

If someone smacks you, turn the other cheek too, I practiced that until I broke. That can't be the right way. Neither can hitting back. I will be like a river, soft, strong, and unstoppable. No one is good or bad from birth. Everyone carries all the dispositions within them and one or the other develops to a greater or lesser extent in the course of life. As the proverb goes: "One man's joy is another man's sorrow." Good and evil are relative and based on the individual. It depends on the observer's point of view.

Everyone is different from everyone else. Everyone sees the world with different eyes. Our view is distorted by the imprints we've received and the experiences we've had. Even a newborn baby is no longer unbiased; it has already spent nine months absorbing impressions in one way or another. Does this mean that everyone can be forgiven for everything? Warmongers, murderers, rapists, manipulators? If you ask "why?" long enough, you will find causes, answers, explanations, and then you will find understanding for every sinner.

It's horrible when I expect others to have the same understanding for my sins, and then they don't give it to me.

I fell in love again and again and ran away from love in return, for fear that it would crush me on the one hand and not be enough on the other. It's only where my needs are really misunderstood (sex?), where I suffer deprivation, that I get stuck and fight for something I can't get. I love where I have no corresponding response to fear.

April 20, 2022: How many NOs does it take to stand up to someone who doesn't listen and, if they do, quickly forgets what they've just heard if it doesn't suit them? I said no five times yesterday up to midnight and I can't be sure. This time around, the person I'm dealing with is not a thug - not like 29 years ago. Yet, I feel my peace of mind threatened. This man can talk without periods and commas, forming half sentences, switching to a different topic in the middle of a sentence, mixing the important with the banal. Feedback isn't received: "Don't interrupt me." He talks all day and night, if he can find an ear to listen. Mine. And then I have to hear him tell me that I can't listen, that I've never been able to do that.

Love's labor in vain. We had our time, met again (we had been friendly acquaintances for about 35 years) when my father had just died and then his mother died. We also both suffered from the death of a brother. We had things in common. But now I don't want my hard-won new self to be talked down to.

At times, it was like a torrent of words made up of wishes, dreams, memories, reports about other people, political rants, detailed descriptions of his work ... . it was no longer possible for my brain to cope.

Let's do this, come along with me there — yet none of this would ever happen. NO. I just said no to everything. What counts for me is what really happens. He still has a lot to do, he's in the red and I've already earned my tickets. I'm frugal and don't need much. My focus is on being and not having. His wishes bear fruit. As soon as one of them is fulfilled, the next wish for something is born. And then it has to be the most expensive whatever. I'm a product of East German upbringing. I don't take on debt. And if I do have to, I quickly pay it off. Not owing anyone anything is one aspect of the freedom I'm talking about.

But thank you, dear life. I must learn to separate myself, to defend my mind, my soul, my body, and my own nest against unpleasant influences. And that's why I've now put several thousand kilometers between us. Since I made the decision for myself, everything has worked like clockwork. I had the travel agency just across the road book my flight in no time flat. I've already checked in for the return trip. On the way there, I met a nice neighbor for the second time in this context. I asked yesterday if she could water my flowers if I ever go away. She said yes and so I had a key made for her yesterday. And today, since the "wish to" had already become a "will do," I met her again on the way to the travel agency. Timing is important in life. When you spontaneously and intuitively follow yourself, doors open and paths clear. If I set my mind to something, I can be very quick.

I need exercise. I've cooped myself up in my apartment for months, looking inwards, contemplating the past and trying to learn from it. It's time to put what I think I've learned into practice. Skin is flapping around my body like an overall that's too big. My joints creak.

The objectives are to build-up muscle, do endurance training, and increase suppleness. A life in the fresh air, on my favorite island by the sea, for once without relationship drama. I can look forward to the future, I'm leaving in seven days. With light luggage, because my tent and guitar are already waiting for me there. There are still over forty diaries to scour through for anything useful, and I'm afraid I've been going round in circles. The stories repeat themselves and become less and less terrible. The development is circular but spirals upwards.

He didn't hear the five "NOs!" either and asks if he can drop by for a moment on the way home to his lonely apartment. And I can feel myself softening ... briefly ... But what for? To connect so we can really part for good now? To call back for a sixth NO? Don't react! Everything has been said a thousand times and I don't want to get confused again or run the risk of telling anyone about my plans. Enough is enough. The cup runneth over. It's shocking how little I'm able to assert myself. Blocked on the net, he still reaches me via my answering machine. I just heard: "You're just mean, dangerous ... , bitch, stupid."

He's on the train and it rushes past, just 11 kilometers away from me as the bird flies. I can already be grateful again that he has shown me what I no longer want to live with. This being unfairly accused and insulted just because he doesn't understand me. In forty minutes, the cup will have passed me by, unless it comes anyway. I should disappear, go for a bike ride despite the drizzle. No sooner said than done. See you later!

I was in the forest for at least two hours before the drizzle turned to rain. Trains were rushing in the distance, and I wondered if it was over now, the cup. Mailbox: "Now I'm a few minutes away ...

and you're not answering the phone, which means you're a selfish pig. I won't hit you anyway, but one day they'll kick you off our island because you're annoying people. Your plans won't work out anyway or you'll retire somewhere, yes, you can do that, but you're just a bitch, a total egotist. Your book is also all about you in the first place. You, always you, always you, the others shouldn't talk, they should read your book, your mother, others, you still haven't got it that YOU are the EGO living in your own world. It's good that your great-grandfather built you a nest, otherwise you would have been thrown out."

Sometimes you must let one thing go so that another can come.

Four hours later, he calls again. It must be terrible for a projectionist when the surface they are projecting on goes away. (If I look at myself, I can confirm this. We love to criticize others for the very things we don't like about ourselves). And the dreamer in him won't know what hit him. We've been separated since the beginning of February.

A little pep talk from a film on Sigmund Freud: "Women are like cigars: if you pull on them too strongly, they'll refuse to be enjoyable." We women are like cats. You must let us come and go. And then, of course, we can also be like dogs, just trotting along. We all have something going on, we're all silly, each in our own way or just sent out to gain experience, feel emotions, learn, grow, become more tolerant. It's all not worth the fuss. Please, let's all calm down for a moment. The world is on fire, life goes by so quickly, and there is so much to do.

"If you're in a hurry, take your time," my neighbor told me, like me, she's suffered her whole life under time constraints.

Yes, I'm selfish. For decades, I've been trying to get to the bottom of myself, to find out what prevents me from being a happy person, even though ... I am happy, happy in my own way. Or do I still place too much value on the opinion of those who say

"I love you" the loudest? Experience has shown that you should trust them the least. They usually say: "Come here and love me." Sigmund Freud said: "Stop thinking about love!" And yet love was and is my absolute favorite topic. If you want to find it before the lights go out in this movie, be prepared to go to great lengths — or not.

Be yourself, be honest, then you'll find what suits you. I'm quite self-critical and write a lot of things down, I've been reflecting on myself since I was 14 ... and I'm not a bit wiser.

I'm a writer and I'm curious to find out your response to my selfish ego. I'm not doing this for my own adulation. I want to help myself and perhaps this can also help others avoid getting a fist or two in the eye from the person they most love.

I had neglected myself; it was too much about the world, the others, now I must help myself. My "car" hurts. Oh, I remember that I had a ticket booked today and everything went so smoothly. I drove into the forest to escape the strange love of my ex-boyfriend, the possibility that he might suddenly turn up on my doorstep after all. Drove to the oldest tree in the area, maybe eight hundred years old. I walked around a bit to make sure no one spotted me, leaned against it, took a deep breath, looked at the ground between my feet and saw a penny there. "Because gold is found in the dirt and roads are made of dirt." Marius Müller-Westernhagen gave me this sentence.

Throughout my life, I've been shuffling through words of wisdom that others once uttered. These clever minds have been useful to me and that's how I would like it to be. At some point, someone may no longer feel quite so alone because I experienced something similar and tried to explain it. Maybe it will somehow help the big picture. Anger is destructive. But we want to preserve this world, protect it, forever and ever! I have children. And what if they want to have children too? I've recently planted an apple tree.

Today is April 21, 2022, and I've just found a really long text with apologies in my mailbox. He didn't really mean what he said. That's a big problem for me, that many people aren't honest and don't say what they mean. How are we supposed to understand each other like that? What to believe in, what to trust? If the first statement wasn't meant that way, how do I know that the second statement is true?

In September 2020, I ended up on the beach close to where he was camped out. He helped me level the ground where I wanted to pitch my tent. As I said, we'd known each other since the 80s. I'd never had any closer contact with him since realizing early on that he was a master of many words that were full of hot air. His plans didn't work out and more than once I witnessed his tent breaking down or being swallowed up by the sea while he was having a beer in the pub talking about a better world or shitty politicians. Or what a great stud he used to be and what great things he was going to do. I knew that his dreams had been lagging behind him for decades. I arrived on Crete a shadow of my former self. I'd just completed my first stint of nursing on a Covid ward, watched my father fall apart, enter a care home where he awaited the TV broadcast showing him getting awarded for special service for the good of humanity that never came. When the care homes were closed and the residents were no longer allowed visitors, my father's world must have collapsed. Having been useful to society all his life, he was locked up, banished, and no longer even visited. In a very short space of time, he deteriorated from an upright, strong man to a broken old man. Alzheimer's and Parkinson's did the rest. When he died, they "refrigerated" him for three weeks and that's how he looked when his wife, my half-sister and I were allowed to see him again the day before the funeral. I can't get rid of that image. The next night, I couldn't sleep and was afraid of losing control of myself at the funeral. I had avoided events like this in the past. I was angry with my employers for not allowing me to have the day off to cry into my pillows. "You already had two days when he died." That agitated night, I slammed the bathroom door and caught the little finger of my left hand between the door and its frame. I have no idea how I managed that. The fingernail was sticking out at a right angle, the top was folded down, I could see the bone.

A huge bummer, but also a blessing. I hadn't even realized how bad I was feeling because of all the stress and worry. I wouldn't be able to work for months.

Family grave. My father had invited me to follow him into it next. When I saw that they were stacked on top of each other: grandpa at the bottom, my brother on top, grandma on top and now my father on top, I found it strange.

Something about me seemed to have died with him. Other people found my reaction strange. Once again, I was ready for the island and started writing my first book for the world. But it wasn't good enough. A lot of things were just too crazy, and names were mentioned, which I now avoid. I don't want to tread on anyone's toes.

So, during this time, this man was my constant neighbor on the beach and fished me out of my doldrums with his fairy tales: "I'm Wolfi and who are you?"

"Little Red Riding Hood from the dark forest."

Or: "I'm the man from the sea, I've been swimming around here for a year now, waiting. Are you the woman from the sea?"

I didn't take the bait and wouldn't let him get close to me. I had to write. The book was finished on New Year's Eve 2020/21. And on my birthday, January 4, 2021, I fell in love with him.

Right from the start, I couldn't tell the difference between truth and fairytale, between real wishes and impossible dreams. I learned over time, but could he do the same? I tried to complete his unfinished sentences, to find the common thread in his speech, if there was one. Hard mental work for me. Just wanting to hear and understand what was really important.

I took him to the room I had for when it was too cold to stay at the beach. He told our friends that he had been drugged, taken from the beach, and when he had come to, he was with me. He told everything differently to make a great story out of it. All lies. Even if it wasn't meant maliciously, it added to our confusion.

Who is this guy really? At first, I took the trouble to take notes like a secretary, noting down things he said that might actually be doable, fishing the main thread out of hours of chatter. To do this, I had to completely set aside my own needs, like a mother does for her children or a nurse for someone with Alzheimer's.

Believe me, this takes its toll. I made things comfortable for us and at night I fled to my cold tent because he was taking up too much space or snoring too loudly. More and more I also escaped during the day because I was overwhelmed by so much "input." I should have kicked him out. That was my mistake. I've never been good at saying no, defending my kingdom and have always given too much of myself. And when it still wasn't enough, I had to endure such tirades, like the one I wrote down the other day. It was far too much. I kept breaking up with him and then couldn't stick to my decisions because he would lovingly envelop me again. Once I had a strange experience: It was at the beginning of the relationship, and he was with a mutual friend and began eagerly and jealously imagining that there was another man in my life. Then he got wasted on wine and fell asleep on the floor.

I was painting my room, went to bed, and then, half asleep, I saw him standing in the doorway, looking at me and leaving again. Or was I dreaming? As if he wanted to make sure I was alone.

How can I get the thread of my story back? The world, life,

and this thing called love are making me sick. I'm burnt out and I'm trying to understand why this keeps happening. Officially it's bipolar disorder and lithium was recommended as the treatment. No pill helps me, what I need is merciless self-reflection.

Please forgive me for saying "I" so much, there's just no other way. I want to save myself, do better and better so that I don't end up in the red.

Billy's dream realization recipe: Dream — Wish — Want — Talk about it (once is enough) — DO IT. It's quite simple! It's helpful to visualize the goal and look forward to achieving it. Of course, things sometimes turn out differently than you thought they would, but it's always useful to try. As the Stones sang: "You can't always get what you want, but if you try, sometimes you get what you need."

Unfortunately, I forgive almost anything and do it far too quickly. Instead, I point the finger at myself and take responsibility. Oh, even for the person at my side who doesn't and can't do that.

Sometimes things were so awful for me that I no longer knew who I was. I tried to find myself in the constantly changing flow of my names and couldn't do it. Then I was Little Red Riding Hood or the Moon Child from Michael Ende's "Neverending Story" and also Mary, Jesus, and God himself. But I was never interested in their story. It just popped into my head. As if ... such self-forgotten people like me are infected by faith, by the much considered thought that prevails in their culture.

I'm ready for the island again and want to finish this book first.

THE WAY IT WAS

Seven months after my escape from the batterer, my incredible naivety won out. I gave up my safety, job, and apartment, was on my way to India with him, got punched in the mouth again and parted ways during a stopover in Aman. There is no reward for too much understanding and forgiveness. This degree of too little self-preservation is punished. In a world where dirty deeds are swept under the carpet in respectable upper circles, I'm traveling on a magic carpet so that light and love can reach my misdeeds or mistakes.

TIME JUMP

After lots of mental work, exercise, fasting for 40 days, a foray into religious delusion, 6 follow-up cervical operations, my escape from a hysterectomy, but experiencing a brief death, I heard a little voice in my head in mid-2000: "Billy, you're not only responsible for yourself. You must eat." Who's speaking? Am I pregnant? I hadn't had sex. One month later, I had a baby girl in my belly. When she was just over two years old, she said: "The next child you are going to have will be a boy with X as the father." A month later, I also had this child in my womb.

Other women have also had future children predicted by their existing ones. That gives you food for thought, doesn't it? There were currently three deaths that were very close to me. We communicated when I took a brief detour into the afterlife. My maternal grandfather wanted me to take care of my mother. My paternal grandmother wanted me to do the same thing for her son, and my brother reminded me that I hadn't yet experienced TRUE LOVE.

A wave brought me back to the beach.

My two children sometimes seem to me as if my father's mother and my brother were in some way inside them. As if their souls had decided to help me in this world full of people in need. After my father died, I became so transparent again, I was half in the afterlife, half on earth, and felt my mother's father inside me.

Before he died, my father said that if he was to be reborn, he would come back into this life and if that wasn't possible, but his spirit was still there, he'd find a way to reach me. And he did.

Not everyone is able to believe such nonsense, but I can and do. The spirit can materialize, you can see that in the illnesses. And that God was able to impregnate Mary is something I experienced in my own body, in my spirit. I also experienced it's possible to die, to continue to think while dead, and to come back to life when needed. I also empathized with God. He just said: "I AM." And by that he meant all of us who are, were, and will be one. He wanted everyone to fully understand and BE that. Completely and truly. In the name of the Father, the Son, the Holy Spirit, in the name of the Mother, the Daughter, the Holy Whore, in the name of Love, AMEN.

October 3, 2020: I've just come back from the island, I'll probably be unable to work for months, my finger is numb and I'm not really sane. Corona and the uproar about "house arrest," compulsory masks, and vaccination, preferably imposed by the state for everyone, is driving people crazy. I want to see that my children are doing well, sort out a few things, then get out of Germany quickly, and hide out at the sea.

At the quarry, almost alone with nature, I was able to let myself drift so beautifully, found little stones and sentences, looked in the forest, thought I spotted chanterelles and realized that they were cigarette butts and lots more pieces of rubbish. I built a kind of memorial out of them. All in one pile. In the end, a shoe fell into my hands. It said: "Your Cleaning Team No. 1." Funny. I put it on top. While I was working, my brain formed a poem inspired by the inscription on my father's gravestone: "Respectful Bow" (you can read in the chapter "Poems.")

As you can see, the story continues. I write for the sake of writing and not so much with a goal in mind. So, it's not about the book on display in a store, but about a kind of self-unveiling. Interesting word. Has to do with metamorphosis. A butterfly is also the result of an unmasking. How do I get in my own way? I want to love and be loved. How does that work?

April 21, 2022: Writing is like conversing with another part of myself or with several different ones. I ask myself something and the answer comes as if it had been waiting for this very question to finally be asked.

Last fall, I asked two children I was friends with at the beach, independently of each other: Which came first, the chicken or the egg? The girl said the chicken, of course. The boy said the egg, of course. This shows how naturally contradictory truths live in different people's heads. No need to argue about it! Maybe one is true and the other is true too. And then there is the thesis above that both are true at the same time.

Another example, borrowed from Shakespeare and combined with Schrödinger's cat thing: You can be or not be. And you can be and not be at the same moment. Got that? The moment can be here and now and at the same time anytime and anywhere. The moment is just like me.

I'm happy to have separated myself from everything that isn't good for me.

Life rewards those who take care of themselves. Since I've been happy, writing has also become easier. As a psychiatrist, I would perhaps assume that a manic phase is on the horizon, but I have a pretty good grip on myself. I know what's important to me and don't buy useless nonsense. The only thing I'll splurge on is travel, since it always has to help me recharge after I've worn myself out. I flee from those who pretended that they loved me. Among other things. Of course, it's also very healing to leave the everyday grind and routine every now and then, where you often forget why you're actually doing all this to yourself.

Why are we here? Why am I here? What can I do for the world? I draw strength from the things that I enjoy doing. What I'm doing now feels meaningful. But because I used to be a work-aholic and moved around a lot, my body is currently suffering from a lack of demand. I need balance. I'm well on the way to refloating the Billy ship. "I hope for nothing. I fear nothing. I am free." Thank you, Nikos Kazantzakis.

"You still want to live, find more people who feel, who know, together we won't miss anything here that still keeps us from going our way. You will see how they murder, how they torture, how they give up their own lives. You will get to know them. Realize what they are really like. You will move on. That isn't your longing." From Rio Reiser — another tender-hearted one.

Life's no bowl of cherries, that's for sure. And only the tough come out on top, only the best get to the West. I don't want to be better or worse than anyone, I want to be enough for myself. I'm doing that and yet I know that it's not just about me.

"Do you really think you don't have any friends?" — Why did this question hit me so hard? Because of the pattern: always having to do everything on my own. No one understands me. I'm not good enough for anyone and no one is good enough for me. As I was never good enough, no one is good enough to help me now. First, I have to realize that I'm fine just the way I am. And also, that I can let people help me. It's impossible to cope with all the demands of life on your own ... isn't it? I'll handle it. It doesn't matter if I'm wrong. Maybe you, as outsiders, understand better what's going on with me. I don't have the distance.

A quote from somewhere, "Me is just another one always changing the other ONE."

Billy Luise Sauerampfer, who are you? Sleeping beauty in a hundred-year slumber? But no! I'm a member of "the Partysahnen,"[1] my own band, of which I'm the only member. But that doesn't

---

1   Translator's note: The band's name, "Partysahnen," is a play on words between party, partisans, and the German word for cream, "Sahne."

matter. Nowadays, with the help of technology, it's possible to put together a whole band ... You are the singer, the harp, the piano, the drums. And you can also be your own back-up vocals. I don't know the technique, but I know the instruments. I'm a musician and who knows, maybe I'll find some fellow musicians so that we sound harmonious together. It wouldn't be the first time. I've already played in a few bands. I have to say that the ecstasy I've felt when making music with others is much greater than what I've ever experienced in terms of love. Desire, freely sounding out what the heart speaks. Let's call it a day for now, because I need to sleep.

April 23, 2022: Courage to part ... Saying goodbye. Then as now, I'm separating, even though I still love him. If I could see myself as a fire, I'd be a burnt out one by now. If I saw myself as a well, then every last drop would have been drawn from it. I know everything about him and don't want to hear anything more. If my mind were a funnel, it would be overflowing with all his dreams, unfulfilled promises to himself, to others, and to me. The trust is gone, his world view is completely different. And his opinion is, of course, the only true one and the rest of us are just too stupid. I can't allow myself to be insulted in the worst possible way just because I think differently. That's not love, it's not even friendship. Even enemies can sometimes agree that they just can't agree. And when someone listens so little, throws all attempts at explanation to the wind, still doesn't understand the sixth and seventh NO, the only thing that helps is to run away. There is no more sign of me. I'm off, far, far away. Unattainable.

I must stop confusing longing and struggle with love, wanting the impossible, loving the unattainable. I'm just realizing it myself. The unattainable no longer wants the unattainable. History is repeating itself. "I don't need anyone" — that's how it started.

That I helped myself when I was three, four, five years old. And I keep coming back to this point.

At the end of the book from 1993, I find two more nicknames: "Tweezer Grasp" and "old Pippi Longstocking," given to me by the children I looked after.

I'm collecting my names. "Little Ducker" ... until 5, "Wee Bee" ... until about 12, and "Little Loon" from my parents. At school they called me "Homie," from age 14 then "Omi Homi" because I'd turned into an agony aunt, from 18 "Billy" with changing add-ons: "the kid," "the king," "Holiday," "she is a panther," "DJ in the psychiatric ward." I was the "nurse who sounds like she's singing," "Anamika Nadi" — the nameless river, "the woman who grasps like tweezers." ... Seen through the eyes of a child, at 26, you're already very old. Last year, someone called me "Old Ocean Lady" and I was already more than twice that age. I call myself "Billy Luise Sauerampfer." My children called me "Billy" for a long time because others did, later sometimes just "Mother." I was "Nurse" to all my patients for decades.

Who am I now? I, that is, another, a constantly changing expression of a being.

I am again the one who wants to come back to herself but is still so inhabited by this particular him. He sends pictures, movies, holds me. I can understand him well, I decorated so much of his apartment. Giant pictures on the walls and perhaps this is the first time he's been alone in a strange place since our trip home from the island. Enough of this. I'm ordering myself back to myself!

On July 21, 2020, my father decided to die after I'd told him the day before that some people just fall asleep and when they wake up, they're dead. His wife then advised him to ask God if that was okay. Not for him. He needed another violent fall to break him, or rather his pelvis. And then he let go.

WHAT HAPPEND WITH GOD ON EARTH

A story. Heard and played back in the style of the "telephone game," or "pass it on."

God came to earth to see how people were dealing with the opportunity he'd given them. He had disguised himself as a beggar. He knocked and the door was opened for him. He was thirsty.

He asked for a glass of water. Somehow the visitor suspected it could be God himself.

"Oh, God, good of you to come. I really need a color TV, a yacht, and a big house to impress the woman I love."

"Man, I'd like a glass of water, please. I'm terribly thirsty."

"Of course, God, you shall have it, but please, it is urgently necessary that you fulfill my wishes first. You'll get your water."

God, who was already used to getting a lot of grief from people, agreed and hoped that he might finally be given something to drink after fulfilling the petitioner's wishes. But NO! The lucky man completely forgot who he had to thank for all this. He watched TV, sailed around the world, invited friends over, impressed them with his house, bragged about his wife until the house went up in flames and all his possessions — including the color TV — were destroyed, his wife left him, and the yacht had to be sold.

"Oh God, what have you done, please, please help me!"

"I can't help you, I'm still terribly thirsty. Where is that glass of water you promised me?"

Poor God, a helpless helper too? This story seems so familiar to me, giving a lot and going away more than empty-handed. Mother Earth is just like that. How many plants, animals, and indigenous peoples have we already wiped out ... We humans are the cancer of the world. The dilemma: If I think we are all one, then I've done everything to myself, I'm to blame, no, I'm responsible.

I've always forgiven everyone very quickly, loved them again, and don't hate them. Even if they've put me in mortal fear. Thank you for the training sessions. Now I must forgive myself for being so hard on myself. Me, the master of my own skill set.

And why am I still not letting them love me? They all just want the best for me. Because I don't love myself? Surely that can't be true. With all my thinking and talking about love, I still haven't got it? Myself, my stupidest student? Hey, Billy, don't be so hard on yourself, just love yourself! But I do that, right?

April 25, 2022: He's still speaking to my voicemail. After some initial teasing and whispering, he slowly gets angry again because I just don't respond anymore. That makes it easier for me to break up. Today I'm a little angry myself, thinking of all the I-LOVE YOUs I've heard, unfulfilled promises, hopes. I know that I am and will be fine on my own. I'm my very best friend, I can rely on myself 100% and, I can respond to my inner child like a father and mother, protect it, comfort it. I have my full attention at the moment and that's the best I can do. I'm helping myself. Right now I'm following Louise Hay's advice and every morning I step in front of the mirror, look into my eyes and say, "I love you." That's funny though. I should say I love me. But as I look into a pair of eyes, I say YOU to me. You are me and I am you and that is one.

Last night I met a woman who I think has gotten herself into a toxic relationship. With a black eye and a freshly stitched wound on her temple, she sat across from me and defended her abuser. Oh, he didn't mean that, he apologized, he's not usually like that. I'm sure he'll never do that again. How familiar that sounded to me. For almost three years I was regularly beaten up and all the well-meant advice bounced off me until his boot almost crushed my heart in the last attack.

Seven months apart, healing, a new life, and a lot of mental work and then, as I already mentioned, what kind of boundless naivety, what kind of enormous self-deception, what kind of hopeless hope only drove me back into his arms? Love, I thought ... How stupid! Such a waste of energy! You learn from your mistakes, so making one isn't enough.

October 18, 2020: My little finger on my left hand is in such bad shape. It's the one I used to chew on in my crib as a small child, by the way. So, I'm on sick leave for the time being. It's the whole Billy package that's not running smoothly. My body hurts, it needs food, exercise, and sleep. My tender little soul is wandering between joy, hope, and sadness. Again and again, I have the feeling that I have really good people around me, friends even, but then I realize that I'd better not have any expectations, that I shouldn't let myself be deceived. Disappointment is the end of deception.

Today I doubt myself. Is publishing this book really a good idea? Written in this hushed, flowery way. Doubt gnaws at me because I fall victim to my childhood patterns and get confirmation of this from friends: "Well, you're better at drawing." Not good enough again, even though I did my best.

October 19, 2020: Thunderstorms, rain, and live music. "What if God is one of us?" Religion is reconnection. Just, I've never had anything to do with the church in this life, apart from Christmas.

HE IS, I AM: Thus, everything that can claim to be, even that which says nothing in this round of life, but nevertheless IS: God, ALLA... AH. Everything and nothing, because nothing IS.

I try to internalize what a part of me knows: I am good, good enough, simply because I AM. And continue writing. If you don't like it, you don't need to read this stuff.

I am searching. I'm searching for the answer. I'm searching for the answer to the question: What is a boyfriend — a partner? I feel like, as my mother predicted, I always fall for the wrong ones and I'm the cow that always gives and when I'm all gone, I'm alone.

An example: I needed a place to retreat to, a room for myself and a roof over my head, at the time I had just completed 40 days of fasting and pure madness. I offered the guy who was operating the disco back then a deal. I'd clean it and decorate it with my typical paintings if I could live in one of the rooms that belonged to it. He agreed. I didn't ask for any money, and I also paid for and provided the paints and brushes myself. I cleaned, painted and painted, tidied up the whole area, and was looking forward to a few square meters of home, and being able to then renovate my room.

When everything was done, he kicked me out, saying, "What do you will you?"

Such a funny sentence in my supposed friend's version of English. He now needed the room for his employees. Such an energy robbery! I can't remember how many hours of work, how much money, hope, and joie de vivre I'd put into this project. The result was less than nothing. I was left empty-handed again, poorer than before, but one disappointment richer.

What am I doing wrong? I had a similar experience in Berlin, at Café Charlotte. I cleaned, painted the walls, painted for a week and on the last day fell off the ladder onto a marble table, which broke in two. You could then put it against the wall as a semicircle. My boss said the table was so expensive that he had to withhold my wages for it. It was all a lie! His employee whispered to me that he had bought it very cheaply.

Always something like that! As long as they can make money out of me, they make a friend out of me. But when it comes to compensation, I'm left out in the cold. How do I get out of this situation? Give up being a victim! How do I do that? Think positively: I get what I deserve! Really? "Do unto others as you would have them do unto you." (Smiley)

So did I deserve to get nothing, even though I did my best?

Do you understand this world?

26.04.2022: A few experiences richer and not a bit wiser. After a lot of digging in the past, tomorrow I'm off again, forging ahead, strengthening myself, looking out for friends, swimming, dancing, laughing, recharging my battery.

Goethe, "Faust I," Mephistopheles: "I am the spirit that always denies! And rightly so; for everything that comes into being is worthy to perish, so it would be better if nothing came into being. So everything that you call sin, destruction, in short, evil, is my actual element. I'm a part of that power that always wants evil and always creates good." — The Lord in heaven: "I have never hated your kind. Of all the spirits that deny, I am least bothered by mischief. Man's activity can all too easily slacken, he soon loves unconditional rest; therefore I gladly assign him the journeyman who stimulates and works, and must, as a devil, create."

Thank you, Mr. Goethe. I also sympathize with the devils, it seems.

I won't be lugging any old books with me, just the current journal — free of old baggage, I'll see what's going on now, what I'm doing. I'm a lucky girl and very good at being in the right place at the right time. After eight months of paperwork and expert opinion after expert opinion, I've finally received my pension notification: full reduction in earning capacity, limited until September 2024. Copied, printed out twice, put in the job center and employment office mailboxes. Let them work out amongst themselves who gets what from whom. I'll let things take their course and be on my way. The way I am, I can't hold any public office. Isn't it good for the system that I'm proactive with initiating my own therapy?

Hey, I sleep at the beach. It still costs nothing. I give myself my swim training, my drawing lessons, my music therapy, dance therapy and so on and so forth. I cost almost nothing because I'm a self-reliant person. Everything self-made — my whole life, because I needed it that way, the hard way? Am I personally responsible — is everything my own fault? No, no, no, there's this inherited guilt that you carry around with you. What your parents couldn't solve, couldn't heal, you now have on your agenda.

As I said, I want to spare my children from running around in circles like their ancestors did. And I still do. But no, that's also mean now. Everyone does what they can.

May 2, 2022: Crete. God created the world in seven days. I rebuilt mine here in five days. 37 years of training as Mrs. Robinson on the beach, at least once or twice a year. I have a small tent. Some people would probably be much quicker, but I just want it to be really nice. The rocks that are or could be stumbling blocks have to be out of the way, as do any prickly things that could hurt my tender feet. I also need a clearly recognizable route or path so that I can find my nest under any circumstances. Sometimes it's dark at night and sometimes well, I'm mentally not all there.

I'm still and always on a course of self-development in the truest sense of the word and the wildest stories have happened to me out here on the beach, I've had the greatest and most terrible experiences, had time for love stories, more or less significant. I died here and came back and shortly afterwards had my first child, the second was also conceived here under the starry sky.

Two days ago, three men were sitting outside the supermarket talking and one of them said something like: "Oh, the hooker ... ," turned to me and greeted me. Maybe he didn't know that I spoke his language. I couldn't get it out of my head all day whether he meant me. Of course, it's not always just about me, but it was just the four of us there and men aren't *putanas*, of course. How many of my dear lovers have insulted me like that, especially when I didn't want to dance to their tune or even when I was breaking up with them? My aforementioned worst tormentor said: "You love EVERYONE anyway. Always spreading your legs." I had meant that I love EVERYTHING, but he wanted to misunderstand, as he was suffering from jealousy anyway. Yes, how funny, I didn't "cheat" on him once, but he often cheated on me. What I think and do myself, I also believe others do. A projectionist at his best.

It's so shitty with people who don't reflect on themselves. They see their own shadow in others and fight against it. And I immediately have to take a good look at myself. I don't know what I'm doing wrong. As an outside reader, you might be able to see through me better. Don't trust anyone, least of all yourself, my mother used to say. She was the first to call me a "whore." I was 16, came back from a trip to a vocational school and had pierced a hole in my earlobe with a safety pin and had a hoop in it. I met her on the street in front of our house and instead of greeting me first, she immediately roared: "You look like a hooker, what will people think of you? This all reflects badly on me and you are in for it if that missing bit of your ear doesn't grow back!"

And him too, my last boyfriend, called me a whore when I wanted to break free from him. He wanted to throw stones at me the next time I saw him again ... And let he who is free from sin cast the first stone.

From the outside, I've loved so often only to once again break up, that you'd think I'd have a lot of wear and tear. From my point of view, I've always dared to get involved with someone and yet I haven't really been happy. Or they were just holiday romances with a foreseeable end. For 37 years, I fell in love again and again on this beach, because it was here that I could be myself.

"All they ever want is my body, they don't want my soul," sang Udo Lindenberg. Yes, it always feels as if no one has ever really recognized me for who I am. Instead, they wanted to enjoy my motherly, sisterly attentions and, of course, the physical attention, but otherwise only have themselves in mind.

Love me, I need you, because I can't do it alone ...

Whore! I would like to remind you once again of my wonderfully corrected prayer ending: "In the name of the Father, the Son, the Holy Spirit, in the name of the Mother, the Daughter, the Holy Whore — in the name of love. Amen." Isn't that fairer?

Basically, the woman should be named first, but since many of us are mothers, let's cut the guys some slack.

What is it that makes men have the urge to forget about women, oppress them or worse? Is it because they were dependent on a woman as babies, or because they would have liked to fuck their mother when they were growing up, or because the latter wish remained sublimated, perhaps it is the cause of many ills? The Oedipus complex the cause of wars? The things that pop into my head …

Incidentally, it was very presumptuous of me to want to be faster than God with my world-building. The punishment followed promptly: my back hurts and I hardly know how to stand, lie, or walk. I wrote in a very awkward position in the tent last night. And perhaps the pain fits in perfectly with the emotionally charged topic I'm struggling with at the moment.

The WHORE was abused as a little girl. Guys, I'm sorry for repeating this, but I'm not done with it yet and repetition is circling through my life. Maybe I'm turning myself into a whore for my loved ones because I hope to get back what I want: respect, attention, and tenderness. To all the men in the world: a woman's whole body is an erogenous zone. We love to be stroked without necessarily having to spread our legs afterwards. We love it when you understand that we understand you. It's really great when you let us talk, and you listen and understand us too.

I'm entangled in a role, empathetic to the point of no longer being able to do anything for the one I love, soaking up his situation, his story, and looking for solutions, helping where I can, building little nests, mending broken clothes, sorting socks, and often eating eggs at breakfast the way he likes them, even though I don't normally eat breakfast. It can go so far that I no longer know who I am, because then I am YOU. If there's not even room for my own thoughts, it's high time for me to hit the road. I kept saying it clearly, but everything stayed the same.

But thank you, it brought me here, to this wonderful island, the sea is roaring, the campfire site is ready, and I've stocked it with wood for the second time. I inaugurated my freshly tiled shower today around the tree that supports my hammock, so that it can be watered at the same time. My friend, the tree.

May 4, 2022: The other friend I'm trying to let go of is still very present in my mind. Finding distance isn't easy here because a large part of our story took place on this island. On my path, I take one step forward and two steps back. How should he and how I realize that IT really is over. I reacted again in a weak minute and opened WhatsApp. And there I found 20 messages the next day. They ranged from "You threw me away" to "Come on, let's sleep together or at least cuddle." A smooth cut, I knew that already, is easier on the nerves and the phone. Unfortunately, my heart and mind don't agree and if I listen to my mind for days or weeks and dutifully avoid contact, at some point my heart breaks out, "... but, but, but I still love him." What nonsense! I've experienced this many times and still haven't learned anything from it.

Because I walk so strangely due to my lower back pain, I've also developed a knee problem: sometimes the kneecap seems to be out of its correct position and I can't take another step, but if I shake my leg out, I can walk again.

I had a crazy dream today: I was on the run from a man, ended up in a hospital room, and found a little old woman — covered in poop from heel to toe, my pursuer was behind me again and said meekly: "That's my mother." I grabbed the tiny woman, cleaned her up, and bathed her in the sink, and while I was washing her, she turned into an infant.

I wonder what that means. Maybe the guy was having trouble forgiving his mother for some shit, and I was giving him the opportunity to realize that she was once a tiny, innocent baby too. Or the dream is supposed to say it's not my job to apologize to his mother. To each his own cross.

My dream, my life. My mother said something like, "You're crazy, you're just trying to be important" when I told her about being abused. That was a load of shit. I thought I'd forgiven her long ago. Of course … her beloved first child had died and she just didn't have her head free for me, but making a liar out of me was still not nice of her. Even later, when my parents had long been separated, she passed the buck to me when it came to any blame: "It wasn't the dog, it wasn't me, so it can only have been your fault." So now I must absolve her of the guilt of blaming me. When I was younger, I felt guilty about everything anyway and this led to an over-responsibility that even drove me to forget myself as an adult and to slip into the role of Jesus with the feeling that I had to carry the whole world on my shoulders and save us all.

The man who haunted me in my dream could well have been my father. Because as I mentioned before, he caused my first mortal fear by pulling me backwards through the Baltic Sea on my stomach. He also put a lot of pressure on me as a coach, father, and teacher. I was supposed to become a world champion. Not only in sporting terms, but also in the fine arts. He also trained my mind. And I'm very grateful to him for all that and I love him. I also love my mother and all the innocent beings on this earth, even those who have brought guilt upon themselves, because they didn't know what they were doing.

But what about me? Why am I so surprised when someone I adore actually likes me too?

Love, this enigmatic being, has been driving me all my life. It's so easy for me to love everyone, but I don't really seem to like myself. I think I'm 100% okay with myself, even if I make mistakes.

So what? Then I'll just learn from it. I'm afraid I haven't gotten rid of the guilt yet. That's why my cross hurts me so much. That's why I still humbly get down on my knees in front of everyone and everything, forgive so easily, because I too have brought guilt upon myself.

But damn it ... what have I done?

In the meantime, I'm my own persecutor, the fugitive, and the little old-world grandma who became an innocent baby again after being lovingly washed by me. Dreams are not lies. It is very beautiful how our subconscious or superconscious speaks to us. I'm very grateful to life and to myself that I now have time to listen. As an advanced adult, I unite my brother, my father, and my mother in myself and ask them not to forget me.

Why did my father respond to my "I love you" with "I love me, too?" Why can't I recognize the love of my respective partners? Love for me, I mean. Sex and desire aren't the same thing as love. If you're used to not getting enough attention, you feel somewhat at home in this state. Maybe at some point you won't want any more attention, not even love. You wouldn't even recognize it.

I have no idea whether everything I'm saying is coherent. The sentences write themselves.

My senses are wide open. I certainly don't lack awareness of my surroundings. I immediately sense when someone is in need and leap into action to help. But I can't see when someone sees me, nor can I see how they might be looking at me — I've made sure of that with my short-sightedness.

The sun and moon shine down on me like a pair of eyes because I squint a little. I feel very connected to the universe. I don't care about geographic borders created by people. I don't harbor any prejudices against any people, "foreigners," because that just seems stupid to me. I ... WE ARE ALL ONE.

Recall please the scientific findings that everything that exists here was compressed into a tiny, highly energetic point of light 12 or 15 billion years ago, exploded and is still expanding. That was us!

May 8, 2022: I was warned: If you think too much about yourself, you run the risk of losing yourself. God and the devil both live in the mirror and have the same face: mine. (You could also say that good and evil both live in me.) Michael Ende said that we are all mirrors in a mirror. So I am you and you are me. Isn't that surprising?

Innocent and naked, in my father's socks and fisherman's shoes, I was sent here, a trainer of love, not to vilify instincts, though I'm strictly against murder — and being murdered. (I've had, well, visions or memories of being murdered three times in past lives: once as a man and twice as a woman, shot backwards in some war, burnt and beheaded, I had these visions when I was not quite myself.) In my case, I have myself on my conscience. Am I the master of my own fate?

The issue was guilt or responsibility. Traumas ... I do think that childbirth is a major disaster for mother and child. There is no guilt ... and the big bang ... do you remember — so torn out of the all-encompassing unity. All of us, who were one, blasted apart to the four winds.

I imagine we are here to learn. There are events and we can decide how we react to them. That's our responsibility. For a long time, I thought perhaps I'd been such an asshole in a previous life and that's why everything that happens to me in this life is somehow justified. How else could my grandfather's rule work, according to which the sum is always a constant? What you take will be taken from you, what you give will be given to you. I repeat myself. AHA, too much is never good. Too much is also bad because it disturbs the natural balance. If a person gives too much of themselves, they inevitably have too little left for themselves

159

and will probably not be able to find anyone to fill that hole. Life often punishes those who overexploit themselves more severely than a thief, because at least the thief has thought of their own self. Me first and foremost. Every mother dog will first eat something for herself before she lets her puppies have their turn. I was only satisfied when everyone else seemed satisfied, everyone was full, all the homework was done, the room was tidy, and maybe I was freshly showered.

Then, in a quiet place, slowly and in peace, it's my time to eat. And then it takes me a while to arrange everything nicely. The individual pieces shouldn't be too big, the colors should go well together. You could almost say I'm addicted to harmony. In the heat of the daily rush, it can happen now and then or even more often that I completely forget to eat and drink. Because there's always something else to do, something that's out of tune.

Ever since I left my school days and school bag behind me, I've been walking or driving through life with a rucksack. As I'm a peaceful warrior, this practical army rucksack is brightly painted. Under no circumstances do I want to advertise for armed forces. In general (like in the chapter "Fool's hands smear table and walls)" I paint everything: my bike, shoes, t-shirts, indoor walls, outdoor walls.

Have I mentioned that I wasn't a good businessperson? I couldn't make a living in the business world. I paint my world the way I like it. Even at 55, I haven't lost that yet — in fact, the opposite is true. I finally have time for my passions and talents.

My life has been an endurance run. Thanks to the particular choices people near and dear to me made, I've often been forced to rapidly pack my rucksack and disappear. As if I'd prepared for this early on, I was an expert at doing a fast-vanishing act. Thanks to the rucksack, I still had two hands free. That came in very handy later as the mother of two children.

Where was I? Billy likes to run away. There were people I didn't want hurting me anymore. I can hurt myself quite well enough on my own, thanks. It certainly wasn't my intention, but since I've been back on the island, one thing has led to another: a blister on my right thumb from raking, a burn on the middle finger of my left hand from making a fire, a painful sacroiliac joint problem from hauling stones, followed by problems in my right knee and, as if that wasn't enough, I stumbled in the dark on the makeshift steps going down to the beach, and landed on both knees in pebbles.

Good for me, because my thoughts were too often revolving around the person I want to forget because he had taken up too much of my inner space. Forget what you want to forget. An impossibility. As the bird flies, I've put almost 3000 kilometers between us, even my place on the beach is a fortress. I practice drawing boundaries.

Pain is a good way to remember yourself. My friend and masseuse said that if while I'm trying to let go, I keep taking one step forward and two steps back, it can easily break my back.

It's like it was almost 30 years ago — and I still can't get away from what is obviously not good for me. It's not his fault that I have such boundary problems. And my love seems to feel most at home in a quite unhappy place. But then again, not really. In fact, this person reminds me of my father, whose issues always dominated the table-talk when I was a kid. This is boring, I often thought. Listening to my father made me never want to grow up. Of course, over the years I've had some good times in various relationships. But when it somehow became too sweet and nice for me, I probably missed the negatives that I remember from my childhood.

How do I get out of this mess now? Avoidance seems to be the smartest thing for me right now. I won't get involved in any romantic story as long as I'm not sure of myself.

Love was and still is elusive, unattainable, with either me or my adored ones always fleeing. I've already said: Life is a joker and plays tricks. Life opens up possibilities, brings other people into the picture, and with them, what was so difficult in the last relationship suddenly becomes very easy. Especially communication, or talking and listening, giving and receiving. I'm starting to change and no longer say: "No, please don't!" when someone wants to help me, but more and more often "YES." Physically, I was so miserable that I even asked for help.

The first saying I learned in Greek means in essence: "The easiest is the best." It's a different approach to "The more resistance, the better, the stronger we become." I'm trying the relaxed approach now. I'm trying to try, because beach living still involves a lot of hard work. Just getting firewood is a major undertaking. But it's also exercise, and I like moving about. It's also about basic needs and being able to start a campfire. That's part of being out here for me. I like to be prepared. All you have to do is hold a lighter or a match to it and it's alight. It could be that musicians are wandering around aimlessly and will gather around my fire. Or something or someone else will come along — or not. I've lit countless fires over the years that I just enjoyed on my own.

There are ways to make it easier for desired events to enter the realm of possibility. When I was lonely, I sometimes brought a second sleeping bag and another pillow.

When we were all facing and dealing with Corona and traveling became impossible, I applied for and received a new passport, packed my duffel bag and yes, I got vaccinated. My reasoning was: I'd already been vaccinated against so many things and if that's what it took to be allowed out again, I'd do it — and it worked. A few days after the border opened again, my sister and I flew into Morocco.

The first time my son tried his hand at fishing, he stood by the sea with a fishing rod and bait to no avail. It made sense to me that he first needed a bucket to be prepared for the catch. He got the bucket and the fish came promptly. It's important to be prepared for what you want to achieve, to be excited about the fact that it might work. But please do so with an easy-going, serene approach, because of course everything can turn out very differently than your hopes and expectations. That's not a bad thing, because everything has a reason and a purpose. That's how I see it and I live more comfortably than those who get upset about everything.

I'm busy taking care of myself, or rather I've done the prep work for doing that. I've collected and arranged flat rocks like tiles on the sand beneath the camping shower bag, hauled water for the bag, got provisions for food and drink, vegetables of all colors, vitamins, and water. Everything the heart desires, no, even more. I'm in a place where my soul is growing wings again. Here I am human, here I am allowed to be. The other Billy, the free Billy, who observes stones while singing in the buff, dances, and finds the peace to indulge in solitude.

May 10, 2022: Becoming who I am is my plan. It still requires some development work. Learning to give up homework, for example. I had put on shoes that were far too big for me and sometimes thought I was responsible for the whole world. Or at least for setting an example that every ME can start with themselves.

There's no God who brushes my teeth in the morning, and there's no devil who causes bad breath. It's all up to me, what's going on right now, and it's everyone's responsibility to make the very best of it day by day. What was, was, what is, is. We sit at the navel of time and knit moments into eternity, turn our wants into actions, dreams into reality. Wake up, brush your teeth, then it will work out with the neighbor and maybe someone will want to cuddle. And if we then become more and more peaceful and harmonious from the inside out, we can also put down our weapons and instead of war and misery, experience utopia. Paradise on earth.

I am close to it, on an island in the sea on an almost deserted beach. The neighbors are on the same wavelength as me, and as for cuddling, there are kitty cats without end here.

HOME?

July 28, 2022: A break-in (to your home) is a break, a break of trust, a break of dawn, and a break in routine that gives you pause. Back in Germany, I'm forced to realize that brushing my teeth and a positive attitude to life alone aren't enough to live in peace with my neighbor. I have a wonderful book by Jiddu Krishnamurti: "Breaking into freedom." But this isn't about such a break-in, but about that break of trust, my naivety, and real theft. While I was away on the island, someone had found my poorly hidden spare key, stolen it, and wandered through my apartment helping themselves to their heart's content. And this someone seems to be my nearest neighbor. A person to be pitied and to whom I'd often given food to because I knew how little money he had. So, I'd opened my heart to him and invited him into my home, apparently so he could get a good idea of what's kept where. I'd bite myself in my own butt if it would help me finally get it into my head that ...

It's not the first time I've trusted the wrong people, tried to help them, or make them happy, given them presents, only to have them turn around and steal from me.

August 03, 2022: I would like to quote a master wordsmith to get to the break behind the break-in. Stefan Zweig said: "To decisively shake a heart, fate does not always need a mighty push and abruptly advancing force; to unleash destruction from a fleeting cause stimulates fate's irrepressible desire to sculpt. In our dull human language, we call this first quiet touch an occasion and compare its tiny measure with the often powerful force that continues to have an effect; but just like an illness is so tiny until it makes itself known, so miniscule is the start of a person's destiny until it becomes fate and portentous event. Always, in the spirit and in the blood, destiny has long been at work within before it touches the soul from without. Recognizing oneself is already defending oneself, and usually in vain."

I know deep inside me that inner processes are reflected on the outside if I haven't been able to resolve them in my mind, that evil appears to me on the outside for as long as I don't welcome it as part of myself. Let's take a look at all the things that are happening right now.

I was in the process of describing a love story that took place 30 years ago: "good nurse meets penniless dreamer to realize a dream together," or "giver meets taker," or "gullible soul meets world hater."

Against my better judgment, I was obsessed with this man and wanted to believe that the power of my all-forgiving love would change him. How stupid. In the end, I realized that it was my own fault. Anyone who allows themselves to be taken advantage of, cheated on, abused, owned, and possessed for years is taking poor care of themselves. The victim becomes a perpetrator of violence against themselves. On a physical level, this manifests itself in the form of this self-destructive illness.

You would think, how nice, she's got it, understood ... But NO! I fell into the same trap again and again. Again and again! I recently had to move out of the apartment I'd been living in with my children for the past 18 years, and I did so full of hope because the old apartment hadn't been safe for ages. Things kept disappearing in mysterious ways. The wind was to blame. If it blew too hard and the windows were open, the front door would burst open and SOMEONE would take the keys ... Again and again, over many years. Of course you're all now thinking: Why didn't she just have the door repaired? I ask myself the same thing. No time, no head for it, no excuse. Our keys were still hanging on the doorframe. It couldn't have been easier. And up here in the room under the roof, I thought I was finally safe, but unfortunately, I had made a fool of myself and opened the door to the thief. At first, I didn't understand, I thought my head was mixed up, that I hadn't yet memorized where things were in my apartment, etched their locations into my consciousness. Only then did I realize: the poorly concealed spare key had been stolen.

There can only be one person who has the motive, opportunity, and local knowledge, but I can't prove anything, only react. The locks are changed, contact is broken off after I'd told this person twice: "I know what you've done." But to help you (and myself) better understand the situation, there were several problems going on at once: the brake on my bike had snapped in the middle of a ride. After the repair, the bike was left well-hidden in the garden in the garage overnight. But the next morning, both tires were flat — not broken. Was it the neighbor again? But that would mean he could get through all the doors here. Or had the repair guy inflated the tires and not closed the valves properly? My personal insecurity grew to the extent that I believed the thief was omnipotent.

"Will it make it easier on you if you've got someone to blame?" U2's Bono sings in the song ONE. Is that true and it's easier for me if I blame someone? Certainly not. It's my life and the fact that the battery in my old notebook has given up the ghost and the new one I bought won't charge is probably not really anyone's fault. It was time, the transience had shown itself, on my laptop of all things.

Transience is also increasingly knocking on my mother's door. Her doctor said: "The good Lord only designed us humans for 50 years." She's 82. Even though we say, "things can only get better," some things just don't get better. Machines wear out, so do people. At least the bodies, which could perhaps be described as cars that drive the spirit soul through life.

I see the signs of the times.

SELF ... Thirty years down the line, thrown back on myself, I ask myself what am I doing to myself and why?

On April 27, 2022, I jetted off to Greece to my favorite beach to get away from a love story that seemed to be all about the other person, or not even about him, but about taking myself back completely and giving all my attention to being me.

I'm telling you (again) that life really is a joker! Even if you change the stage and the actors, you can't escape yourself or the story, the educational tasks you must overcome, the lessons you must learn.

As soon as I arrived back on my favorite island, another man began coming on to me: "I want to get closer to you, Billy, I want to give you shelter ... " Shelter — him to me? He should have warned me about himself or warned me about myself. End of the story: He's a sorry ass and depends on people paying attention to him, admiring him. He was only interested in me somehow succumbing to him, being interested in him, while he basically couldn't care less about me. He showed this, for example, by coming on to me, making sure he had my attention, only to leave me at my little spot on the beach, ignore me, and move on to the next victim. He'd managed to reel me in, I believed in love again, let my heart break three times until I gave up. In the evening of the same day, the other man — the love? — that I'd left back in Germany because my energy was being drained dry, turned up on the island, too. After four months of separation and heartache, he was so familiar to me, my mind was blown away. Defenseless, I flew into his arms. Poor, stupid Billy! He had learned, worked, and thought a lot. Now everything would be different, he knew his mistake, he wasn't allowed to talk so much about politics and this and that and who's who.

Yes, exactly, I want us to be here in the now and live, perceive each other, feel each other … , but basically nothing has changed.

So, what have I achieved? Consoled myself with an impossible love over the loss of an equally impossible self-destructive love and then the other way around again. So I go round in circles and am alone with my great empathy like always. Right. When I reflect on my father, my love for him, it was the same there. He wanted to mold me in his image, to make his dreams come true: become better and better, devote all time, energy, and attention to sport, do what he wanted, think what he thought, strive to reach his goals. I should become a world champion because he hadn't managed it. No wonder I was never good enough. He wanted to be the world champ. His disappointment in himself was what I felt all the time that had created my leitmotif: "I'm not good enough, no matter what I do."

I had a similar experience with my mother. I couldn't replace the lost son, no matter how short she cut my hair. She says I was always the good child, unassuming, adaptable, a ray of sunshine, but apparently it only seemed like I was shining.

At age 55, I'm still not a bit wiser. I got into the habit of sensing other people's needs and reacting accordingly, often playing the clown at home and later at school. I'd be the butt of my own jokes, play the fool, so that the others had something to laugh about and then hear them say things like: "You're always in a good mood." How can that be? I'm a melancholic, but in this sad state I'm rather alone. I want to be an optimist, which was hard even back then when you were in the know, and it's even more so today, you just have to open your eyes. We recently celebrated Earth Overshoot Day. We consume 1.75 earths a year. Water is disappearing without a trace, it's too hot, there are fires everywhere, one pandemic follows another, and to top it all off, people won't stop warring with each other. Fear and terror everywhere and the movies on TV try to outdo the actual horror.

Yes … , but life is beautiful. There is this now between before and after. Just as people think the devil is in the details, I believe that happiness is also located in this space in between … . In other words: God and the devil live in the mirror, in the reflection of ourselves. They can only be seen in the mirror, from the outside, as different. They are united within us, good and evil, happiness or unhappiness. How we look at things in life is what matters. I've decided to be a happy person — despite everything — and to accept things that I can't change. And the other things too. Where I find litter or garbage in nature, I take it with me. At least that way I keep my path clean. It's the least I can do to save our planet. And I want to be positive, make people happy, make them laugh, because laughter carries the soul over abysses. I'm a conglomeration of quotes, I realize again, and thank the sages whom I can no longer ask if I may quote them, and whose many names I can't possibly remember. THANK YOU!

The other day, I was hunting a mosquito that was filled with my blood, and just as I slapped my hands together and killed it, the TV chimed in: "Billy, what are you doing?" I felt addressed, even caught: I, who usually saves insects, was a killer. But yes. Break what breaks you!

I "suffer" from magical narcissism, the childishly naive idea that everything I encounter is a mirror of myself. I take coincidences seriously, so it's not surprising that in the very next movie on the same evening, a Billy (played by Brad Pitt) wanted to lead his team to the World Cup. Yes, that's what I want too, my father's ideals continue in me, and I've passed them on to my children. We are well on our way. My daughter paints masterfully and surfs like a goddess, sings with the voice of an angel, and delights her friends with her refreshing, sensitive manner. My son used to draw, wrote songs in English, has taught himself Greek, can dance and sing (he just doesn't know it yet), is becoming a fitness trainer with a focus on health, and stood out in his class with his anatomical knowledge and much more. We are all driven to do something good, to make a difference, to leave something behind that is bigger, that lasts, that helps others, that makes their lives more beautiful. Why? To boost our overly modest egos or really for the sake of a good cause? The latter, of course.

Going back to the coincidences, the happenstances. As described in "The Prophecies of Celestine," the more often it happens that the world speaks to you, the closer you are to yourself, the closer you are to your own truth. To quote Herrmann Hesse again: "It does not depend on what and how much a person reads, but on the happenstance nature of what they read." It also depends on the coincidence of what is heard, seen, noticed, thought, and inferred, about and from happenstance encounters, injuries, accidents, break-ins, and illnesses. Before something can become externally visible, there is first a long internal process that takes place in the world of thoughts and feelings.

I've been typing for five hours, finally I'm working again. A dam has broken.

What do I want now? I'm striving for change.

The day before I flew to the island and following a long battle, my pension was approved due to a full reduction in earning capacity. I had simply reached the end of my tether. A psychologist certified that I was totally exhausted in all areas of my life. I had enough diagnoses to show and my psychiatric report for the pension fund was likely so dire, that I probably should no longer be set loose amongst the general population.

Repetition: The nicest compliment my father ever gave me was, "You are a positive point in a negative world." And so, I kept looking for and finding the negative, for example as a nurse. You are needed as a nurse, but all the gratitude you receive from patients is never enough to restock what you are giving of yourself. The money you are paid for nursing doesn't even come close to adequate compensation and neither does sometimes getting time off in lieu of pay. On top of that, we nurses must distribute medicines that at times are obviously not benefiting the patients. For example, just think about the drugs people take over years to lower their blood pressure. Those of us on the front lines must often get a liter of water into these hypertension patients in no time flat just to try and get their circulation to work halfway properly again — and all the while, having to document the entire process. The mind boggles when it comes to antidepressants and other psychiatric drugs. All in all, you can easily get the impression that the supposed desire to heal is accursedly hypocritical. People are made ill by the therapies that are supposed to be helping them while caregivers, doctors, and Big Pharma are either eking out their livings doing it — or making another fortune. Doing this broke me, and I've stopped acting against my own good conscience. Most nurses are characterized by a certain selflessness, which is why we keep on working even though we are exhausted or sick ourselves. Helpless helpers!

It's a similar story with single moms. No little breaks make the situation easier; weakness is not allowed. Fulfilling the children's needs is the first priority, and once they are finally standing on their own two feet, they start taking their anger and disappointments out on you, act hostile towards you, and we moms are expected to be thankful for the great trust they place in us, to love them no matter what, forever...selflessly, of course, it goes without saying.

I scold, I'm angry, and realize that I don't act differently in my supposed love relationships. Forgive to the point of no return, understand what others have on their minds, comfort the one who hurt me. But now I've had enough. Above all, the thing that bothers me is that I'm the one who has been doing this to myself. What I allow, I do to myself.

I now have a great "new" avoidance tactic I'm trying out. I'm spending more time looking at insects, flowers, and stones — and staying away from people as much as possible. I feel more comfortable surrounded by nature and there, you'll sometimes find a few like-minded people. Almost all of whom are working in the "human support" industry.

Save yourself if you can.

It's very hard to get rid of childhood patterns. I don't need anyone.

It was only later that I realized how much I offend those who truly mean me well when I reject their offers of assistance, especially when I know how satisfying it can be to help someone.

In Greece with a woman friend, I started accepting offers: "Would you like coffee, Billy?" "No, but yes, gladly." — "May I help you collect firewood?" "Well, fine, but what do I owe you for that?" ... I'm not completely sober anymore and shyly realize that it's my film that's playing here. With all the charity and self-sacrifice, I had only one thing in mind: to become who I am. Now, but really, it's about me. A poem of mine: I am only one sound in the world's sound, / a painter's brushstroke, / just one pause to take a breath / I'm simply ME. / Another, / constantly changing, / improving changing / world brushstroke.

I'm not sure of myself at the moment, but I think I suspect that I'm the one standing in the way of my own happiness. How do I free myself from these evaluation grids? I'm as good as I can be under these circumstances, but I'm also pretty angry that I didn't defend myself very much. "Love yourself and it doesn't matter who you marry," popped into my head by chance while I was having sex with a disillusioned husband. And I gave this book to the couple after reading it myself.

Love yourself. How does that work? If I'm out in nature or absorbed in an occupation, if I have my senses open, if the question does not arise at all, then I'm one with what I perceive, with what I do ... and full of joy, contentment, quiet. And then I love all of us, all of our universe with me in the middle of it, as part of it.

September 24, 2022: I just reviewed what I've written and found quite a few repetitions. I can be forgiven!

2022, AUGUST 15:
BREAK-INS ARE BREAKS

A few days ago, just past 10 p.m., I noticed that my cordless landline phone desperately needed recharging. Its charging station was still in the old apartment. So, I sped down the stairs and unlocked the door. It was almost dark, the street lamplight was falling through the kitchen window, and there was the neighbor standing opposite me in the twilight. It took me a few seconds to realize I'd cried out in shock ... and then I began ranting: "Dude, what are you looking for here? Now I've caught you red-handed. But now I know for sure that you've been the thief here all along. Get out!" In the end, my rant was so intense that he ran down 64 steps and even out of the house.

I've already mentioned that a series of break-ins is currently taking place and also that things are breaking down, brakes, battery, recently on a tour with my son, my bicycle bell broke at a slight touch. "I guess I still haven't heard the bells," I thought to myself.

I have constant quarrels with my son, he loves to criticize me and improve my way of expressing myself, the greenhorn. Now that I'm paying extra attention to how I say or write things, I'm making one "wrong word choice" after the other. He just has to pick them out — like choosing an egg from an Easter basket. The lengths people will go to, to make their loved ones happy. And this is the crux of the problem: the constant correction triggers me. It confirms that I'm not good enough. My son reminds me of my father, I just can't please him. He's understanding, explains to me that sons want to feel better than their mothers, and suggested that I stop always getting offended and give in, but rather pound my fist on the table and assert myself. This story with the neighbor ... how quickly I thought of his poverty, almost ready to help him — instead of thinking about myself, the betrayal, and abuse of my trust.

Fate with its "desire to sculpt rages on. Yesterday I learned that my mother was in the hospital, she was suffering from heart and kidney problems and was undergoing heart surgery today. I slept very badly, worried, and prepared myself to give her my care and help. This morning I woke up with severe lower-back pain.

Elsewhere, fish are dying in the Oder river on a massive scale, forest fires are raging worldwide, millions of euros have "disappeared" due to fraud schemes involving Covid tests, conditions in Afghanistan are catastrophic, and so on ...

"Have a nice day despite it all!" I must move, race my bike, swim, get out!

When my father's health worsened, he fell down more due to Parkinson's, and Alzheimer's was taking away his memory. In one of his clear moments, he told me that I "didn't have to do that," (meaning bathe or wash him) because as a nurse, I had enough people to take care of. He was also a little afraid for his dignity if his daughter were cleaning his behind — and he "had an accident." In the end, it happened and neither of us had a problem with it. He's been dead for two years and I'm glad that I did what I could for him.

My mother called me in a panic. Her way of asking for help was to create a silly poem (it rhymes in German.) "I'm not human. I'm not an animal. I'm a roll of toilet paper. Can you help me?" Sure, of course!

My father's death didn't leave me unscathed at the time. Somehow, I flew a bit into the eternal hunting grounds and dissolved, briefly had the feeling of being Willy, my mother's father, was in a lively exchange of ideas with my own father, who said to me during his lifetime: "If it's true that we are here forever, I would like to start right away with this and be reborn as myself." It sounds crazy, right?

Well, I am in psychiatric treatment. Nevertheless, I can't be dissuaded from believing what I perceive to be true. In an old family Bible, I found out that my father's grandfather had the same handwriting as I do. I put it this way in the poem shared a few pages ago. To repeat "Repetition": I am only one sound in the world's sound, / a painter's brushstroke, / just one pause to take a breath / I'm simply ME. / Another, / constantly changing, / improving changing / world brushstroke. I; WE ARE ALL ONE.

September 15, 2022: "Your gifts are your tasks." I recently found this written on a tea bag label. I've had a piano piece on YouTube for a while (Stay at live... Billy) and a completely painted room with a description online ("The Net and the Way Out", Billy), but haven't gotten very many reactions yet, a total of eight likes. What does the world want from me, what could I give it that would be of value? Texts? Again and again, I fall into a tailspin, somehow am not getting further along — like with this story, because I can't get rid of this stupid pattern of not being good enough. I know how idiotic that is: Everyone is unique and as good as it's possible for them to be. There are always better and worse painters, pianists, writers. Life isn't a competition, although I grew up with the message that it was.

My mother needed her daughter's support, and as a nurse, I'm good at giving it. I believe I have the gift of adapting to others, but I realize that I'm no longer able to cope with how I'm doing it. Very quickly, I lose sight of, or don't really know who I am, feel exhausted, drained, oversensitive, thin-skinned. Then I just want to be alone. But I was there for her with my knowledge of the meds and their side effects, until she got rid of the fear and took her life back into her own hands.

September 19, 2022: "During Corona you had to hide your cough," begins a new joke from an Austrian comedian whose name escapes me. But the punchline goes, "Now, if you aren't coughing, you have to hide because it means you've secretly been heating your home." How funny and how not. After a recent spell of warm temperatures around 30C/86F, I was now freezing at night as the thermometer was going down to 9C/48F. Dressed in an undershirt, long T-shirt, sweater, and fleece jacket, I lay in my bed and was finally warm. Energy prices had already increased painfully before we stopped getting gas from Russia, and now heating costs are set to rise fivefold. It's better to dress warmly. In the luxurious country of Germany, we have it super good, comparatively speaking. Yet, people can't get rid of the fear, first of Corona, then of a Third World War, and now of unaffordable heating, poverty, and cold.

Fears, existential angst. I don't want them. I avoid the news and discussions about politics, have somehow put on blinders and stick to the immediate, to what I can really change. Being at peace with myself is the beginning. It's not that easy. I'm otherwise a person of action, I know about the magic, the power of expressed wishes, intentions. They strive for fulfillment, for completion in reality.

I've even put myself under pressure and already told many people that I'm writing a book. Trick 17 with self-deception. It's never been a lie, because I keep writing in my journal, but this first book for the public is so hard for me. The sifting ... what is true, important, what is good? What I write corresponds to my perception ... Important? I've also brought stuff to your attention that is not good.

If you watch the current news on TV, almost none of it's good...

and after the non-rosy nightly news, comes sport, the lottery numbers, the weather. Well, since that's the way things are, then I guess I can complain about the bad things.

I will slowly feel my way back to my central theme here. What is it that I really wanted to say to so many people, and not least of all to myself? The more we take responsibility for our lives, health, and happiness, the more our lives will be shaped according to our wishes.

I've booked a one-way ticket to Crete. This gives me two options: I can come back at any time, and I can also stay for a long time for now. Once again, I'm in a situation where I'm escaping the evils of home. On the beach in my tent with my daily salad, I can live both healthily and frugally. As a newly retired person in a new apartment with utility and extra costs not yet known to me, I prefer to play it safe and live almost like an ascetic.

Change of subject: This comes to mind because I'm trying to save money on everything. My mother recently told me how they used to do it "back then." There was a severe famine. My grandfather was sometimes on the road for days to provide food for his wife and three girls. I remember him saying: "There used to be more eyes looking into the soup than out of it." (In German, drops of fat in liquids are called *Fettaugen* — eyes of fat.)

I'm in a state of mind ... that's so detached from the day-to-day stuff, rather all-encompassing and believe I've realized that everything that happens, whether classified as good or bad, has its logical right to exist. A friend of mine keeps going on about and back to Adolf Hitler and can't understand why people followed him. I believe Hitler is already a star in the firmament, beyond good and evil. It is a fact that he provided work, thereby feeding the people and many were just grateful that there was finally something to eat again. We all know what else he did, we were told about it at school as children, so often that I'm ashamed of my country of birth. I'd rather be a child of the universe.

For a long time, I believed I was a victim, then I believed that in another life I'd surely been the perpetrator, and this time round in the film of my lives, was getting my just desserts. Now I remember again that our destiny isn't ours alone, but that we were given "things" that our ancestors couldn't sort out as homework engraved on our cross. Family homework, so to speak. The goal of our family homework seems to me to be to once again create a family in which a father is a father, and a mother is a mother and together, peacefully and to the best of their knowledge and conscious help their offspring set off into the world. But for this to happen, each of is allowed to and indeed must first reflect and ask ourselves: "What is it that I want?" I'll put it bluntly: I wish to live great love.

My mother gave me this: "If you're not happy with a situation, change it, and if you can't change it, just change your attitude towards the situation." The greatness of the love I'll live is up to me. I've given up believing that one day someone will come along and with them, everything will be fine. That would certainly be too boring for me. Always peace, joy, and happiness. I'm not used to that. Arguments are important when you're close to each other. It gives everyone the opportunity to come back from WE to ME and reassure themselves of their own point of view. We can be different, perhaps we complement each other precisely because of our differences. We are allowed to have different views; as long as one person doesn't want to impose their "truth" on the other, that is good and logical. We can love each other, even if one thing or another about our loved one gets on our nerves or is incomprehensible.

Let me give you an example: I had the following problem with understanding musical tones. As a child, I thought that tall people had the darker voice colors; so for me, high tones were the low tones. Quite logically. It took a while before I was able to clear up this misunderstanding for myself. I fought so hard for this truth of mine. And again and again in conversations with others, I realize that I'm looking at things from the opposite point of view. Never mind. Viewpoints and opinions are a dime a dozen, and the truth is a whore or a weathervane in the wind.

HEROS

Once I read a story that described five successive generations of a family that had lived under changing governmental regimes.

Yesterday's heroes were today's enemies and tomorrow, they'd be heroes again. Heroic deeds decreed and celebrated in one army became condemnable atrocities in the next one, and that changed again and again. No flag, no matter how it's designed, justifies the mass slaughter of our own kind and all other living beings on this planet. Why do we still need wars? Clearly, it's about power.

But isn't it slowly dawning on everyone that we humans are killing off all life on Mother Earth, that people must unite?

Isn't the level of suffering high enough yet? I guess not. Marx was apparently right when he said that a revolution only breaks out when stomachs are growling.

We are simply doing too well.

What can we do, YOU and ME?

I collect garbage and litter wherever I go, just like my mother. I'm sure that this awareness has rubbed off on my children: Even seemingly small actions help the big picture. I'm a lifeguard and save insects, thinking of Gandhi who said: "If you save one life, you save the whole world." A friend replied to this statement: "If you save your life, you save the whole world." Exactly! That's why I'm on this ego trip now, reading my life and hoping that by the end of the story I'll have freed myself from my entanglements, liberated what I've repressed.

It takes a lot of energy to banish something to oblivion that hasn't really been forgotten. And it's hard to let go of childhood patterns.

RETHINKING IT

We are not without power.

From where is the light shining / and where does it lead? / What is life's meaning? / That I AM. / That I am, / me and others / wandering joyfully, / transforming and improving / the brush-stroke of the world — ME."

We have the power to change ourselves, we have often fallen and risen again, stronger than before. Many people have woken up and, like you and me, are here on the world stage for a reason. We are the Peaceful Warriors. We are an army of Peaceful Warriors. We want to live and let live, so that everyone is fed and has a roof over their heads.

We want Mother Earth to live on, to leave our children and grandchildren a world in which it is possible to live.

Politicians are talking about a turning point and want to strengthen the military.

I'm planting seeds in the earth for more life.

2023, JANUARY 1: HERE WE GO AGAIN

I found the following sentence: "Imagine if someone wanted to know your past in order to understand how to love you." Oh no, I thought at first, who wants to know all that, that would almost be too much of a good thing, let's leave the love thing for now, I don't trust myself there, I'm just quite exhausted on the way back to myself.

But, hey, imagine it's me, it's me who should be interested in my past so I understand how I have to love myself or how I can learn to allow someone else to love me. I'm on a roll. It's not new, but it takes time and constant repetition for realizations to work their way through all facets of the self and bring about fundamental change.

I confuse longing with love. Since I've lived with this feeling since I was very young, it now feels like home. I'm used to wanting the unattainable, maybe I wouldn't be able to cope with real love. I'll try to avoid realizations that are just repetitions, but might not succeed, because roughly speaking, my past is a story of repetitions. Repetitive vicious circles, you might think, but it's not quite like that. I learn something and the next round of repetition isn't quite as bad. It goes in circles, but there is a recognizable upward spiral. Not everything is the way it used to be. Because I have learned. Because I've learned, whatever happens, I come back to myself and that's where I'm at home. I'm good with myself alone. I don't have to prove anything to anyone — not even my love.

I would like to talk about my current painful symptom, because maybe it will show me the way to healing. I'm left-handed. And my left hand has been injured for about three months now. It particularly affects the middle finger, its base joint. So, this hand has already brought quite a bit of pleasure into the world by calming down various boyfriends so that peace could be found with them. Do you get where I'm (or better said they were) coming from?) To be more direct: When I wasn't in the mood for sex, but they were horny, the nurse in me found a way for us to get along. I'd take his "cross" or "burden" in my left hand and jerk him off — as the expression goes.

In fact, I often betrayed myself for the sake of peace, doing things that I thought others wanted me to do. I was just wired to please others first. And to be honest, it's an uplifting feeling when someone loses it because of you, or because of your physical functions, achieves bliss and then falls asleep satisfied and satiated right next to you. Great, I've managed to make someone happy again, but what about me? I've successfully isolated myself at the moment, locked my boyfriend out of my life. I'm tired of watching other people break down, destroy themselves, steal my peace of mind by constantly blaring in my ear how bad the world is. I want my strength to be of use to myself now. I need my own help!

January 4, 2023: I'm now 56 years old and excited.

At the beginning of the year, the news anchor said: "We won't be able to stop the glaciers from melting, even if we could slow down global warming a little. We must be prepared for floods and violent storms. I wish you a healthy and happy New Year!"

I found the news on Instagram that the Earth, which normally has a vibration of 7.8 hertz, has been vibrating faster and faster since 2020 and now reaches peaks of up to 60 hertz. Mother Nature is sweating, poor dear. My goodness, what to do? I try to counter with serenity the state of anxiety that grips me every time

I look at the state of our planet's health. Easier said than done. Our world has burnout and anyone who can feel, feels with it. But hey, I'm an optimist and try to optimize what needs to be optimized: first of all, myself and my view of things.

Many people are currently traveling along the same path. We want to quickly reassure ourselves of the eternal (just now, a door here slammed shut), at least believe that we will always exist forever, constantly changing so we can exploit all possibilities. Everything strives to evolve, learn, and keep getting better, just like me, and that's why I've just planted a row of apple trees. Saving, healing, repairing, making a masterpiece out of a (hot) mess ... You can always do something, keep your own path clean, for example, or, as I'm currently trying to do, do what gives me the most pleasure and that I have a certain talent for: juggling with sounds, colors, and words. The gifts show the tasks.

If I can raise myself to a higher frequency by eliciting joy in this way, I can make others vibrate higher and am therefore a useful member of society. I grin and think of my father, whose maxim was always to serve the people, to be useful. "Joy, beautiful spark of the gods ... ," I hear my inner self singing. It often speaks to me in this way. Sometimes I don't really know what's going on with me. Then I listen to what song is ringing inside me, pay attention to the lyrics, and then I know.

So, joy should be my path, taken with cheerful serenity, despite everything and precisely because the overall situation is so precarious. Love life, live love. I feel like I keep coming across this sentence at every corner these days, and I thought I'd invented it. (Just kidding.) We all feed our spirit from the same pool and these truths are there for everyone. Or are they?

One step forward, two steps back. I keep looking back. Yesterday I found an interesting change in my perspective: "I no longer seek adventure so far out in the world, nor wisdom so close to

189

the stars. Neither the past nor the future weighs me down. I was fertile and with the birth of my daughter, a switch flipped in my brain: I will have a future here in this world, the earth will keep turning and we will not perish ... because I'm a mother."

But now I can drift off again, search the past for treasures.

1996: Wherever I am, I want joy to arise. I've discovered a super filling station for myself: faith in love, life, meaning, eternity, and myself. I'm busy conjuring up a ground beneath my feet, on which I then continue, step by step, to follow my path, mine! Is it possible to be free as a couple? I want to be independent in my decisions. I'm the kind of person who always talks about free love because I experienced love as a gilded cage and split up again and again because somehow it wasn't possible to be free as part of a couple. As soon as we had sex, we became male and female, and a stupid sense of ownership set in. My darling, now you're mine, now we're "US." More and more of the ME was discarded in favor of the WE, until I no longer whistled and laughed, painted, or sang, and disappeared without a sound.

I want to be alone a lot. Alone with me, I find myself again, and also joyfulness, then life is as beautiful as I make it.

I've dragged my dignity out of the cellar, and I enjoy and share the strength that comes from peace. I want peace and I can achieve it, every day anew, for myself and my fellow beings. Life offers endless opportunities to do what's yours to do. I'm a "Schwester" (German for "nurse" and "sister") with body and soul. I'm in agreement with what I do and what happens to me.

But sometimes not: I'd given my dog into the care of my aunt while the violent situation was going on in my apartment. I'd evacuated my dog so to speak. Now my aunt reports that he's constantly being victimized and was recently bitten again. He's so scared, and apparently radiates his fear and thus, attracts aggression.

I haven't gotten rid of the fear yet either. Today after the late shift, I was cycling in the rain in the dark on almost deserted streets. A van came towards me with a guy inside who looked at me and made obscene gestures with his tongue. Resolutely, I rode on and passed him. He turned around and followed me. I took a shortcut across Bismarckstraße towards Schillerstraße, but he was already very close to my house. He flashed his headlights. Of course I was terrified, my heart was pounding in my throat. I got rid of him, but I wondered whether I attract guys like that. "Hey, I'm so nice, are you the dog that wants to bite me?" And here I was thinking that this kind of crap was behind me now because I've reformed. But that's not the case. Life is constant training on all levels of existence.

Here's what happened next: I got into the bathtub and tried to get rid of a wart on my index finger when, unnoticed, my left middle toe got caught in one of the holes in the overflow protection and wouldn't come out. The toe became thicker, hurt and fear had me in its grasp once more. By now night had fallen. No chance of calling anyone for help. So, I gritted my teeth and freed myself, or rather my toe, but not without injury.

What does that tell me: If the violence doesn't get to me from outside, I'll inflict it on myself?

The cancer is such an auto-aggressive story and only appeared after I'd left the aggressor.

What am I doing to myself? Am I the director in my movie or not?

Found in "Women who love too much." … "To love too much is to be consumed by a person to the point of self-sacrifice, to equate that obsession with love, to allow it to determine your feelings and much of your behavior and still not be able to let go. It means measuring the degree of love for another person by the degree of torment associated with it."

I admit it, I'm one of those people who loves too much. How do I find the golden mean? Time will tell. The will to change has followed insight.

A patient said to me today: "You look like a DJ." My reply: "Nope, I'm more of a dancer." Another responded: "Yeah, you're out of line." Ha-ha, exactly.

LOVE PARADE ...

Over time, I've realized that going to parties as a way of connecting with people just doesn't make me happy. I'll go to a party alone, make a few eye contacts here and there and briefly feel like I'm on the same wavelength as someone else. Then I'm alone again in the hustle and bustle of the city. I want to get out into the world again. My father was a wanderer and it's in my blood too. It's rare here to find birds like me, plagued by wanderlust and driven by desire to experience the extraordinary in special ways. But first work as the means to an end. Then I'm free enough and take the liberty to buy a ticket and fly off.

Life is, hey, let's be honest, life itself is life-threatening: Last night, some fancy Mercedes station wagon pulled into a filling station — and did it by turning directly across the cycle path — and the lane I was in. I just managed to brake, but my front wheel crashed into the car's right rear wheel. My knees were weak, I was shaking, and the handlebars were crooked. Then a person came up to me who'd obviously seen the whole thing and asked me if I had any money to spare for him. Nobody said life was a walk in the park. It's not for cowards and it's full of opportunities to wonder about people's dealings with each other and the world.

What do I want? To pursue my passions and abilities, to get better and better, to make music, dance, draw, write, talk, listen, learn, express myself, exchange, give, take, grow, help where I can, change what I can, accept circumstances that can't be changed, and make the best of them.

I've spent the past 10 years trying to find out if my partner was someone I could go on a journey with, but I always started out alone because it wasn't the case. Traveling brings you so close to nature and your own nature, releases energy, and breaks down barriers in your brain. I look forward to the sunny days, but also to the darker sides, such as hunger, cold, rain, storms, and loneliness, in short, to the whole spectrum of life — as unpredictable as it is out there by the sea.

What could possibly happen to me? I love life and death is the flip side of the coin. I like being with people who understand and appreciate that time and the ego — as in the conscious sense of self — are our chance. Our destiny isn't just a logical consequence of the past. We humans can think and imagine a better future, look at possibilities, choose, change our path, separate ourselves from companions or find some, or even travel alone and realize that we don't stay alone for long. To each their own. Do what you want. Make a wish, believe in it, say it once, and act on it.

The simplest magic trick in the world.

I'm getting ready: I've mended my rucksack and stitched my fanny pack. My work as a nurse earns me the means to realize my dreams. I often go dancing at night and I'm on the Paradise Productions guest list because I've painted a few pictures for parties. All's good. Things are progressing. And of course, I've already found another unattainable projection surface for my wild feelings of love. It seems to run like a thread through my whole life: I'm always in love, and preferably, with someone who is unattainable. Then I can dream about how wonderful it would be and not run the risk ... What isn't can't be bad. Nothing creates nothing.

It's an avoidance tactic that's supposed to protect my shocked heart. And yet, like everyone in love, I go through hope, doubt, and emotions, and from heaven to hell. And when I can't tear myself away from such a dream, it's high time to travel. I've booked a one-way ticket to Goa. Hurray! I'm allowed to stash my belongings in my mother's cellar. I travel light and burn all my bridges. Tegel-Amsterdam-Bombay-Goa — that's where the road leads now.

India ... Far away from home, I realized that I'd already found a certain circle of friends in Berlin. And this for the first time after 10 years "relationship boxes" where I'd been part of a couple, and friends had fallen away more and more. I was determined not to go back to that.

Yes, Goa offered encounters with like-minded people, surfing, parties, campfires under a full moon, highs, and the corresponding lows. You can travel wherever you want and never escape yourself. My emotional rainbow ranges from extremely happy to deeply sad. Post from my father: "Dear big daughter, your longings are like strands in a spider's webs, incredibly stretchy and tough, they always let you go home and then tear you away from your duty (in the broadest sense according to everyone's circumstances) to ensure the preservation of our species. Take care out there, stay strong. Perhaps you will manage to convince yourself that you can also work as an apostle here in our region. There is always room for it, and you would be welcomed with an open heart. And — there's a need here too."

After some initial homesickness, I found a companion and immediately fell in love again, which resulted in a phantom pregnancy, against which I measured my feelings. Is he the one I want to start a family with? No. From then on, I was the unattainable one and finally broke up. After two months in Goa, it was back to Berlin.

And of course I was immediately on fire again for the unattainable DJ, to whose music I could drum and dance so beautifully. I didn't really want to have him. It fills me with joy to see him, and with sorrow, because I think he doesn't see me, doesn't like me, and maybe that's not true at all. A lot of things have already happened. I painted him a T-shirt, he recorded two tapes for me, and even gave me his address. I'm so blindsided when affection comes my way because I seem to want the following to continue to be true: You don't love me. Stupid, isn't it? Yet this one drummed with me and even filmed me once.

As I didn't have my own place or a job, a friend let me stay with her and I soon made my next travel plans. Within a month I was ready. Equipped with T-shirts and paints, I jetted off to Crete.

By this time, I was on the verge of insanity, somehow leaking out of my fontanelles (those "soft spots" on babies' heads that fuse with time.) I was writing poetry like mad.

My problems always come with me and so I found an unattainable lover here too. They are everywhere. It probably started when my brother disappeared. Maybe I want to prevent someone getting as close to me as he did back then only to leave me again. My father left, my first great love stayed behind in the GDR, and I don't want to be untrue to them, the list has grown longer, unattainable people like me?

That's not true either. (The following sentence is true; the previous sentence is a lie).

It's often easy for me to really see other people, I can empathize. But when it comes to myself, I'm often faced with a conundrum. There's always trick 17 with self-deception. I want to love and be loved, and then again, I don't … out of fear of the echo? I love you. Fine, I love myself too. Or: Great, then you're mine now, just do what I want, and we'll get along great. You? You're not important.

The beauty of these non-stories is that they neither begin nor end and the space in between is as elastic and tenacious as the spidery strands of my longing, ah, father!

After a month as Mrs. Robinson on the beach with campfires, dancing, singing, and falling in love as always, I landed back in Berlin just before the Love Parade. I had exactly 2.98 D.

-Mark left, but a lot of painted T-shirts that I began distributing to people. Just unfortunately, I was far too modest to ask for money. Just buy me a glass of orange juice or a meal. I'm learning and not giving up. And I haven't been able to sleep properly for a long time. The animal is awake.

Because of my maladjusted condition, I sought advice from a trusted doctor, a homeopathic one with years of experience under his belt, meaning life experience. I told him about my phantom pregnancies, my urge to make amends for my family history, my concern for humanity and the whole world, and the occasional bouts of religious delusion. After all, during my first phantom pregnancy I'd had the impression of being Mary, as if a spirit had entered me and wanted to materialize inside me. I currently had a kind of "total recall" going on in which world history passed me by, rather the history of mankind with its genocides, crusades in the name of the Father, and wars and blind destructiveness in the name of Mammon. How desperate. It was whispered to me that I was the one who would have the child, the one who would show the world the way. Why me, it couldn't be me, me wallflower from the dark forest who never believed in God? Too much honor!

It grew for four months and turned out to be a giant cyst in my uterus, a bubble that could talk.

Dr. X took time for me and removed this huge responsibility from my shoulders, explaining to me that in every generation, every person had a part to play, had to carry the cross. I didn't always have to do everything alone. Sepia ("squid") was the right remedy for me. He helped me a lot, especially with his open ear.

I was in turmoil, couldn't rest, and on the day the Love Parade was due to begin, I rode to the Victory Column at dawn and started walking around it. The traffic was gridlocked, there was space, and I was alone.

As daylight came, so did people, more and more of them, and

some of them wondered what I was doing. I want to get over myself. How many more times do I want to go round and round? Until I can't anymore. How many times? Until I don't want to be able to anymore! Later, someone let me drum up a firestorm on their very good instrument and I thundered away with my bare hands. Someone gave me a rose. In the meantime, the square was packed. I had difficulty maneuvering my bike through the crowds.

Love parade, Billy-be-love, now in love with two unattainable guys who live about 3000 kilometers apart as the crow flies and only play a role in my thoughts, who might even like me, but unfortunately, I can't or don't want to see that. I run after them like a puppy, but beware if they turn around or just want to walk towards me, because then I take flight.

A very creative time. Sleepless in my mother's apartment, who wasn't at home at the time, I batiked T-shirts and painted them, at night on the balcony, seventh floor, on Hansaplatz.

It was July 21, 1996, around 1:30 am. Near the Victory Column, to the right of Alexander Platz, a bright "star" appeared in the sky, coming closer and closer, an unknown something, round, spotlights all around its belly, it flew towards me and then left over the house towards the Turmstraße. What a pity that no one was there to confirm what I saw: a UFO. Enthralled by this impression, I wrote the poem "Me" in a flash, as if someone had given it to me.

When I was still able to sleep, I'd dream I was standing on the summit of the highest mountain far and wide and was fishing, just like when I was a child, only with a stick and line — without a hook. Of course, I didn't want anyone to get hurt if they came over in my direction. If young, looney Annette is fishing on the roof of the world, with a never-ending line on a stick, her fish must be able to fly.

I'm feeling the urge to write a book. Here are a few possible titles: " We're at the helm, Mr. Fisher," "It's today," "Nothing and everything," "How Nathan became Jonathan," "A drop from God's inkwell," "The way out of the spider's web," "Primer for the sensitive," "All lies and yet true," "Beyond good and evil," "The beautiful beast," "Semitones in the sound of time," "Childhood patterns and model children," and "The butterfly's dream." I don't have the time or peace and quiet for that. I paint and clean and do things and write in my journal anyway. I want to go to the sea again.

I've cleaned, renovated, and painted Café Charlotte and decorated it to achieve a lovely ambience. It took about a week; I reckoned it would earn me 600 D-Mark. On the last day, I fell off the ladder onto a marble table that was supposedly so valuable that I had unfortunately forfeited my right to a wage. What was I supposed to do as a moonlighting painter of colorful pictures? What is it about me? Is it written on my forehead: "Will do anything/everything for nothing?"

A letter from my (all of our) father: "To you, dear big daughter, a warm greeting with a few stamps, without which the post moves nothing, and the German version of Alice Walker's poem, "Only we can devalue gold."

My father understands me after all and perhaps he likes me a little. I've understood that money in this world is the means to realizing dreams, but I give away the fruits of my talents too easily and cheaply. I've been robbed, I've let myself be taken advantage of, I've been deceived, disappointed, and I never stop learning. I love my mistakes; they make me human and capable of development.

My mother accepted my help as a cleaner and nurse and paid for it, knowing that I was in financial need. She told me that other values were important at other times: loyalty, kindness, durability, serviceability, being class. She said that you got what you wanted because it looked like what it was, unadorned and true, things and people too. Nowadays ... we are constantly made to fear that the world is coming to an end and at the same time believe that material goods can make us happy.

I want to live again and do it with nature on the beach in Greece, that's where I always find myself even if I start out as a drop in the sea.

The never-ending story continues. I'm losing faith in my healing powers, I'm not entirely at ease, I can't seem to get the love for myself going inside me. I feel like the Childlike Empress in Michael Ende's "The Neverending Story." She's threatened by the omnivorous nothingness unless someone comes along soon, listens to her, and believes in her — reawakens her faith in herself and the power of love. In my case, cancer is the name of this nothingness, this void. Every year I dutifully undergo another surgical procedure for my female genital tract. My uterus reflects the state of my hope for an intact world, true love as a free and deep friendship without possessiveness and jealousy, without violence and empty promises.

Father writes: "You will have noticed that the writer also keeps out of life, not just plunges into it. When what is more important is undecided ... "

What I want from my parents isn't a place in my father's or mother's house. What I want from them is the confidence that I have, had, and will have my place in this world. And another kind of blessing: "You are good the way you are." Cutting the cord, the zillionth time.

I'm terrible, sometimes funny, full of energy, wonderful, then again very grim, so much so that my mother didn't dare speak to me for fear I would blow up. Basically, I'm sad and melancholic and need places to retreat to for regaining my peace. If not, I get into a lot of trouble and can be quite explosive. I've always been good at suppressing and controlling my anger, but I'm probably reaping the rewards for doing that now in physical form within my own body.

1996: AUGUST 13 ...

On August 13, 1961, construction of the Berlin Wall began in Germany. History repeating again. Walls were built, jumped over by the free, wild, and untamed, later torn down completely by the sensible, until someone didn't like this new freedom because they feared for their power and wealth and therefore erect a new wall. The walls that you can't see are treacherous, the ones that block our brains when we are children and want to create our own thoughts. And what's with the national borders, shouldn't we be allowed to roam freely on Mother Earth like other proper animals? But what about the limits on understanding, on toleration, and tolerating frustration? (a nice concept, right?) If you've reached the limits and don't want to lose your mind, you need a good dose of humor, as it can really transport your soul over abysses.

I got into a fight with my mother because my so-called blunt honesty, or rather perceptual disorder, memory distortion, and egocentricity, had crossed the line of what she could tolerate. My perception is different to that of others. I've noticed that often. For me, I'm right, I've been reflecting and writing since I was 14 years old.

Egocentric ... it's not the first time I've heard that I'm self-centered, but I give everything for those who are close to my heart, and give myself as well, all for nothing. Oh, that's so wonderfully ambiguous. I'm certainly more or less a combination of opposites: an order-obsessed, chaotic person, a selfless egoist who always has to reflect on herself in order to then selflessly be there for others again. I often hover between this world and the next, crazy and normal, flying high and diving deep.

CARRIED AWAY

Soon, I was loaded up again with T-shirts and paints and back on Crete ... In 1996, the sea had me back and it was more of a home than Finsterwalde or Berlin had ever been for me. The people there greeted me warmly. After all, I'd been living on Crete off and on for 11 years, or rather, my being had always romped around in the same little bay. I was there for two months, the children called me "little mermaid," one guy called me "little angel," and when a fisherman asked me what my name was, I told him that different people kept calling me by different names and I couldn't remember. Then he said: "I call you Maria."

Nature's bosom is such a beautiful way to recognize what is really important in life. Food, drink, a roof over my head, and love that always travels with me. I also received food for the spirit: "The Prophecies of Celestine." This book showed me once again that I can't be that crazy, that I have a fine antenna for coincidences and what's between the lines, the devil in the details, the good in the bad, and how words or thoughts can manifest themselves. And the more you play with coincidence, the more it is drawn to you and gives you wonderfully astonishing moments of wonder.

After just five days in Berlin, I booked my next ticket to Crete because I didn't know where I could stay without being a nuisance. The plan was to visit the doctor, get some warm clothes and, above all, ask my dog if he would rather come with me. To this end, I dragged my friend's giant dog crate to Berlin, which made the journey very difficult.

I will never forget this scenario. I met up with my aunt, who had taken good care of the dog, in a large meadow. The three of us first indulged in a great joyful reunion. Afterwards, we set off in opposite directions. The poor animal was torn, running one way, then the other, barking, howling, and deciding in favor of the rescuer and a safe cozy home. I was the one who had let danger get to us, and I was the one who had left, and it was never clear what was in store for me next, and therefore for mine. Our dog had made a good choice. I jetted back to Crete with the empty box — big enough for a giant Schnauzer — worked feverishly for very little money with my Greek friends. I had another earache, too much money for dying — but too little to live on.

Today I quit my waitressing job and told the boss that I'd only worked for a week so I could pay the doctor. "I don't care," he said, "I gave you the job because you needed money, I don't need you." But I can see that I was a useful member of this working community. Everyone has to do more work now: the waiter, the women in the kitchen, the friend at the bar.

I'm so rich on the inside. But in this mean world I can't manage to give the right thing and be appreciated accordingly. I keep falling into the red, emotionally, financially, and physically. Not to mention that I think I understand everyone because I can put myself in their shoes, and now this anxious question: Can anyone in this world understand me? Is anyone interested in me at all or is it always just about the others?

No wonder I'm self-centered. Who, if not me, would concentrate so much on themselves, or me, if I don't?

Nobody.

But there was somebody. When I had no more words, I ambled around the tavern, from table to table, asking for opinions, suggestions for improving this world of ours, wanting to send them to the Pentagon, to the Council of the Wise in this world, but I was already well on the way to slipping into a dream world again, had a fever. One of them wrote: "A knowing whiteness in her eyes looked at me. After a brief inward freeze, I surprised her with the glowing yellow honeydew melon in my arms. Enchanting! A kiss from her luscious lips brought cheerfulness to the circle. Since then, one of her eyes shines yellow, the other shimmers wilting white. For you, you my little wine grape!"

Perhaps coincidence will have it that you see your words printed in my story.

On October 25, 1996, I was back on Crete with the dog crate. What a back and forth. Where am I and above all: WHO? I'm looking for a truce within myself between light and shadow, innocent and guilt-ridden.

Sorry, I take responsibility. I know that there was a key bad experience in my life that was the reason for my strange but not funny love and relationship career. I've known it for a long time, and I keep repressing it and then I experience something similar so that I may remember it. To remember that I must protect myself in this world, to separate myself from everything that isn't good for me.

It's not easy.

Found an interesting text (but no longer am sure from whom. Stefan Zweig?) It says: "The misery comes from the fact that everything that is called religion today is mechanical convention and repetition. When an original creature really experiences their gods and sees the invisible in the flesh, as happened in genuinely religious times, it arouses the unease of conventional worshippers. For nothing upsets time, which is itself only a dull copy, of an original."

December 1996: After days of inner turmoil, I pulled the world map out of my bag and let possible destinations pass my mind's eye. Where would I go?

I had a dream: already on my journey, I'm standing in front of a departure schedule and eagerly looking for the next date to return home.

What is that supposed to tell me? Child, you are a refugee, uprooted, it seems.

Egypt, India, Israel. Again and again, I was looking for people I could feel comfortable with, and yet I remained a stranger. And well, as a woman alone in a foreign country, I was also constantly on the run from people, especially men, who were all too intrusive in wanting to make my acquaintance.

My thirst for travel, my wanderlust, is understandable when I think of how long I could only dream of ever seeing the sun from outside the zone behind walls in East Germany.

But while traveling, the longing also grew to arrive somewhere, to lead a normal life after all, to play father, mother, and child in a safe home, in an intact world.

I'm driven ... the world isn't intact, and neither am I.

Running for my life, trying to heal myself with fasting and yoga and other wild physical tasks that I set myself: crossing the whole bay from right to left until the sun goes down, always trying to overcome myself. To understand the psychosomatics of my disaster, I follow Rüdiger Dahlke and Thorwald Dethlefsen and the book "The Healing Power of Illness."

And as an aside, yes, I feel the urge to leave behind something useful that could make this world whole again.

What should that be? What can I do?

Save myself. 1997, I'm 30.

What was up with you last summer, Billy? We're hearing all kinds of stories about you.

Armed with the above-mentioned book, I came to Crete and began the book's recommended method. I had to remember all the illnesses I'd ever had and then think or check back on what had been going on around me at the time with family, school, etc. To be clear, I started a fasting cure. I didn't have any money anyway, so not eating suited me. I wanted to unravel myself, find the root of the evil cancer, and understand my strange behavior towards men and love.

It was an exciting journey! I could no longer sleep and soon my consciousness split into three entities. There was Annette, reviewing her life along with illnesses and feelings. Then I was also a being out of time, falling from one role into another, remembering terrible experiences, murders of the worst kind. I was burned alive, beheaded by a guillotine, and as a man on the wall, got shot from behind. And then I had the voice of an old man in my head accompanying me and announcing my next steps: Look at the experience, feel your way into it, but don't worry, it won't be as bad as it once was.

And of course, I can't leave out the fairy tales I resorted to when I no longer knew who I was: Little Red Riding Hood in the dark forest, the Moon Child from the Neverending Story, the Little Mermaid, I found myself everywhere ... and I became the good Jesus.

Whenever an experience from the present life was censored, not accessible to my consciousness, I first remembered something much worse from another movie. Pure madness and then again not. Phil Collins sang especially for me "Billy, Billy don't you lose my number, if you are not anywhere, how can find you?" So did Manfred Mann with: "Wild Billy was a crazy cat." I could find myself in everything but was also lost in everything at the same time. The letters the Greek postal worker left on the counter in the pub for their recipients to collect[2] all seemed to be for me in the sea of changing names and roles.

What could I do but finally come to the realization that I AM.

---

2   Translators note: Mail in this part of Greece is not delivered directly to recipients' homes or businesses.

Wait a minute, that's what God is supposed to have said. If that is the case, if I find myself dissolved in everything, then I am one and everything and nothing and also God like you.

Dissolution and megalomania. As said, I had nothing to do with religion, but religion also means reconnection and basically all religions, myths, and fairy tales are very similar. We were expelled from paradise, we are no longer one, but we are. From stardust we became individuals who can say "I," but through this realization we fell out of the paradise of ONENESS. You and I, good and evil, light and shadow, all pairs, just like life and death, which basically belong together. Separation is an illusion that causes great suffering and longing. GUILTY and it's our own fault. In India, a Shiva Baba advised me to keep my hands off the spiritual worlds. These weren't to be touched until one had planted a tree, built a house, and raised children. Around the age of 51. Forty nights without sleep ... In between, I was once drugged with sleeping pills by friends and my mother in a team effort, which robbed me of the rest of my trust in "my people." Of course, everyone always only wants what's best for me. Just I didn't understand what was wrong with me. Despite everything, I'd had the feeling up to then that I was still in control. Now, I thought I was dying.

I was trained at and worked in a psychiatric hospital, so I knew that religious delusion is the first sign of endogenous psychosis. I'd also dealt with two people who were convinced they were Jesus Christ. It is an illness, a madness, says psychiatry. But perhaps it is also a special spiritual experience because you understand at the same time, we're all resurrected. It certainly wasn't my idea to remember world history as Mary, nor to feel responsible for everyone and everything and the whole world as Jesus, and to have loaded humanity's guilt onto my back, my cross. The path to God, me as God, was the humorous answer to the despair of not knowing who I am anymore. But I am just as much God as plankton, it's not megalomania, it's rather humbling. We all, the sum of the whole, are the philosopher's stone.

Developmental steps: I want to become a mother (Mary) I'll take over the responsibility (Jesus) I AM ... (just like everyone else.) But surely Mary thought that sex was somewhat dirty, AN-IMALISTIC. And then she used her knowledge of physicality and since she'd been chatting with God the whole time anyway, she simply transformed the spiritual energy into matter. Einstein was a good friend of hers. How did Joseph feel about this story? Surely, he knew this commandment, "Thou shalt not commit adultery." Did he really believe that his wife had been impregnated by the Holy Spirit? Was he already so far removed from any instinctive reasoning? Well, maybe so, and maybe not.

The expulsion from paradise began when we became aware of ourselves, when we stood out from the animals. The monkeys must have flipped us the bird and said we were crazy.

This business with Mary's immaculate conception is so misleading. So abstinence isn't the best contraceptive after all? Mother! What have you told me? Anything can always catch you out and the best contraception is to just be prepared for anything with a kind of open serenity.

A philosopher's stone, which came first, the hen or the chicken?

Illnesses, for example, prove that feelings and thoughts can manifest themselves so that what needs to be considered becomes visible. If it's skin, it's about boundaries, if you have skin problems, you have boundary problems. If your ears hurt, there is something you don't want to hear anymore. Mary wanted a child, was attracted to a man who obviously didn't fulfil her spiritually, and so she didn't let him touch her body, but wanted so much for her faith, her love of life, to manifest itself somehow, and she managed the magic trick: to become pregnant INNOCENTLY.

As a woman, you can find yourself in a pretty ugly conundrum: You're the mother, the saint, the lover, the whore, the best friend, the guilty party ... "And what else can I do for you?" How long has that been going on? "And you gave them everything, your strength, your youth, your life."

Eve ... evil ... devil ... Shiva, now I've got it: Eve bit into the apple of knowledge. She, or rather the realization that she was her own being, disturbed the peace. So, women and the awareness of their own, individual selves are to blame for war, and they also give birth to soldiers. Which brings us to childbirth. Is it not again the woman who destroys the unity between herself and the child by giving birth to it?

Which brings us to sex. Now, which man didn't want to mate with his mother as a young boy and then again didn't and got into hot water over it? And then later, the woman is the seductress, drives him crazy because his animal instincts drive him towards her. When it gets too much for her, she blocks it. The woman has the power to permit activities to preserve the species or not. At the same time, she is also the guardian of death, she sits on the threshold. From there she receives the children and with every menstruation she releases the chance of a life on earth. Women are frightening. And again, usually it's women who care for the dying and accompany them in the process of death.

And what about men? How are they doing? Seemingly not very well, either. Once, they were hunters in the wild, useful because they brought in food and at the same time, they could let off steam physically and form social bonds with their own kind.

I feel like a woman with masculine qualities. I've always been able to get my food on my own — and often, for the man in my life, too. Primarily, I'm just a person, so the name BILLY suits me very well.

I had closed myself off, I see that now and remember my

213

summer mistrust of humanity itself, and I mistrusted myself the more I realized how unworldly my experiences were: Being Mary, Jesus, God himself. Somehow there's something about letting your ego shatter into 10 000 shards for once. After all, you can start all over again afterwards.

I dream of emigrating because the values that are important in Germany don't suit me. Life flows by far too quickly in Germany, distraction is the order of the day, time is money. Everyone seems caught up in their daily routine with no time for, and no idea of themselves or other dimensions. It's all about having, not about being, often about superficialities, soccer, soaps, the weather, and in the same breath about wars and disasters. Then people rant and rave about their neighbors they can't manage to live next to in peace. I had no time in Germany and no strength or nerves after work for friends or myself.

April 1997, Crete: My heart was on ice because I didn't want to lose my temper again and then retreat into my snail shell in disappointment.

Now, after making some inquiries, I've got the go-ahead to fix up the only stone house on the beach for myself. I'm already in the process of clearing out the garbage and two capable boys and a good friend are helping me.

I'm tired of being so exposed to the elements. The child needs a roof over her head and windproof, non-see-through walls for protection and some privacy. Putting up some boundaries in a place that otherwise tends to encourage either blurring boundaries, are doing away with them altogether.

Dissolving boundaries has often happened to me, but this was the first time I lost myself in everything.

In the end, I solved my riddle and collected myself again, recognized who I am here and now, at least roughly, despite everything, the shock is still in every part of my being. You could say I accidentally went through a kind of reincarnation therapy, splitting myself into the entities I needed for it. Fortunately, no one put me in a loony bin or sedated me with pills. Many of the people around me were at a loss and would've gladly had me committed to an institution. I was loud, I was annoying, scary, a disaster. No wonder. I can understand myself. I dreamt: I was walking through meadows and fields with a friend. A woman and her husband were working on one of the fields. I was still thinking, how nice for them to do something like that together when the man came up to me, threw me to the ground, and assaulted me. I struggled to fend him off but stood no chance. I looked around for my friend, who had just carried on walking, screamed for help, but nobody reacted, even the man's wife just kept on working on the field.

Change of scene: Suddenly in a kind of camp where women were held captive to serve as whores. Shocked, I asked if this was a dream, what year it was (around 1000), tried to make it clear that I didn't belong there, that I was in the wrong movie, that none of this could be true.

In another scene, I was at a concert with girls and my current heartthrob was apparently singing and playing just for me. So beautiful to watch from a distance. And he came to me, went into a room with me alone. Nothing worked anymore. Unpleasant tension built up. Completely rigid, we couldn't talk or do anything else, the air became too thick to breathe, and I just wanted to get away. An illusion and its end.

It was just a dream. I'm here in sunny Greece, everything is green and blooming and what can I tell you, I'm in love again. That's what worries me so much.

I've successfully let go of the two unattainables, but what if I just change the projection screen and get just as lost as I usually do? I was warned: "He can't love." Great, that's fine, then I won't run the risk of being loved, everything will be the same as always.

Oh, Billy ... was with him yesterday and had a severe panic attack today with shortness of breath at its finest. I thought I was choking and luckily, we found someone to take us to my friend's house. She had Aconitum D6, which helped me calm down.

Anxiety and the fear of anxiety can really get to you.

I no longer know how beautiful love can be or whether I would be able to cope if someone reciprocated my feelings.

Basically, I'm not worried because I know all about deception and disappointment ... Little Red Riding Hood from the dark forest has just learned that you can't trust wolves, that it can end badly if you get involved with them. So somehow love is this wolf, it can unleash the wild animal in him or me, which I'm not entirely comfortable with. Love drives me to do things that are extremely embarrassing when I look at them from a rational perspective. I've already crawled on all fours over hill and dale at night to get another "get lost, leave me alone" from my beloved. And the things I've put up with from men in the name of love are beyond belief. What I've let them do to me! My fundamental trust is in tatters, so I prefer to flee, avoid real contact, and often lose myself in daydreams.

C.G. Jung comes to mind. I make the logical mistake of thinking that if the wolf in one story has eaten my grandmother, then another wolf in another story will do the exact same thing.

I'm on guard and first look to see what is real and who this person is that I believe I'm in love with now.

First of all, I take care of myself. I've found a nice campsite. I've found a job and I'm doing breakfast service in a bar. On my first day, I was completely overwhelmed. A whole group came and wanted breakfast, fruit juices, freshly squeezed of course, various types of coffee, omelets. Fortunately, 90% of the people staying here are friends or at least acquaintances and a friend helped me in the kitchen, teaching me how to make omelets just the way the bosses wanted. In the afternoons after work, I can swim, which I love, or continue working on the house at the beach. I've already found some hard-working helpers.

Life can be beautiful. In the evenings, I go up to the tavern's roof terrace, where it's quieter than downstairs, and continue painting T-shirts or keep writing until this book is finished.

At night I dance in the disco or the bar, or drum the beat to the music from the speakers, or light a fire on the beach, which always attracts musicians.

Making music together is better than sex. When you've found a harmony and we all inspire each other, rocking higher and higher, it can lead to a state of ecstasy.

The wolf has found somebody else. Fortunately? Yes. I must learn to trust myself first. Sure, I'm a bit jealous, but I like them both and I don't begrudge them hooking up. I behave extremely stupidly when I like someone. I chase after them, I'm there, but I don't offer them a target. I avoid talking to them, I avoid getting close to them, I just give them the cold shoulder, or I attract attention by suddenly leaving. Great tactics!

At least I've learned that I can let go of what doesn't want to be with me. And the two lovers asked me nicely if I was okay. We are friends. By the way: I lost my necklace while swimming in the waves (A dog who's freed itself from its collar.) In the morning my watch stopped (wants to tell me that something is over) and later, while building the house, I found a watch that was still running. This place seems magical to me, especially when it comes to finding and losing things. Everything balances out so quickly here. I've been paying attention to coincidences, signs, and symbolism for years.

I also work on my own healing, as my physical manifestations symbolize my mental and spiritual dilemma. So, I build stone circles or spirals of white stones, each of which stands for something, for something worth striving for. For every insight I add something. If I want to get rid of something, I look for a stone that's as big and heavy as the problem. Then I throw it as far away from me as possible into the sea, and say, "Wash yourself first," or "I certainly don't need you anymore!"

"Miracles are not in contradiction to nature, but in contradiction to our knowledge of nature." (St. Augustine)

The more I believe in miracles, the more miraculous things happen to me. And I know how I can bring about miracles. Making wishes clear, formulating goals (or anchoring them in the material world with symbols, manifesting them, as I do,) and visualizing how wonderful it will be to have achieved what I long for. And feel joy about it and then get going with it.

Life is a joker. Love again, and once again, two unattainables at the same time. The one I thought I'd let go of turned up just as the other elusive bubble burst. Isn't that a miracle? I find, "In each you see only the reflection of what you decide he is to you... Dream softly of your sinless brother uniting with you in holy innocence."

Before I fell asleep last night, images flashed before my mind's eye: a small dog in a bucket of water, circling to the left, then becoming a baby, spinning faster and faster until the image became a spiraling mist. That is probably the fate of us all. From spiral nebula to spiral nebula and being born again and again in between. Why do I torture myself so much with my little life on earth?

It's like this. I can be alone. I know my way around. It seems to be the animal instinct of wanting to preserve my species that keeps blinding me with such pretty, rose-colored glasses. It can even make me feel afraid because it robs me of control, splits my heart and mind, which means I no longer trust myself. Love is a state of extreme confusion, wildly torn between hope and doubt. At least I have enough faith in myself and in life to believe I'll experience what I need for my development at the right time and in the right place with the right people, even if I don't like it at first.

It's stupid that I somehow think people don't like me, even though I hear it often. A friend helped and said I could just go for my goal. It would be worth it.

And it was worth it. I brought the Greek god down to earth, reached him and lo and behold, he was a person like me who you could look in the eye and talk to. Confrontation therapy. The fear was an illusion.

THE DARK SIDE OF THE MOON

Fifty years ago today, Pink Floyd's album "The Dark Side of the Moon" was released. It is now 2023.

At the moment, I'm getting lots of flack about writing this book. It shouldn't be too personal, and above all, I shouldn't publicly tell stories in which others are blamed.

I'd like to point out once again that I see life as a boot camp in which I encounter my unlived, repressed shadow from the outside. There were certain traumas, overcoming them only made me stronger.

My parents were also traumatized, as they literally walked over corpses from the time they could walk until the tender age of five. Dead bodies were lying around in the street. The horrors of war burned themselves into my ancestors' souls. What did that do to them?

Each generation wanted to do better, to improve what it didn't like about the previous one. I'm not trying to pin the blame on anyone. I do have understanding. Everyone can only work with the tools they have at their disposal. What were high values yesterday are no longer valid today or have been replaced by something else. While our parents were driven to impose discipline and order, today it's more about individual freedom and emotional sensitivities.

Fortunately, I haven't experienced a war up close yet, apart from the fact that social media can almost give you the impression that you're actually watching a war live. What is my small suffering compared to other fates? A fly in the ointment, not worth mentioning? Suffering is a way into deep layers of the self, leads to knowledge, compassion and enables us to recognize happiness. I thank life for every dark experience. So that I may emerge from it shining brighter.

Every person who ever touched my heart is part of my heart and moved me, made me grow.

When I preached freedom, I found someone who taught me about it.

The last boyfriend was terribly jealous. Now I've found someone who made me feel my own jealousy, wooed others in front of my eyes, and made sure again and again that we were still happy. I learned my lesson. For seven years, he loved me at the beginning of the season and then all the others.

I'm telling you:

LIFE IS A JOKER

And probably, I'm still not really capable of commitment and found myself friends who are either in the same boat, or they live so far away that real closeness is almost impossible.

There were also times when I threw love around.

"Who's going to cry if you break up when there's someone else around the corner?" That's how my mother comforted me over losses in my teenage years. As mentioned, I was tempted to put it to the test, to try out the wisdom that came to me in my life.

My stays on Crete were a wonderful training ground, because the fact that the vacationers jetted off back to their lives at home after two to three weeks limited a love story from the outset and averted the danger of things getting too serious.

"You're afraid of wanting everything, of getting everything, because you're afraid of losing everything again." I saw this on TV. Maybe that is exactly the kind of coward that I am.

My first great love was the deepest and completely without sex. It was friendship and yet love — like between brother and sister. Later, I saw him love others and he loved me too. Jealousy was nipped in the bud. Friendship grew and with it understanding and compassion. If you really love, you give your friend all the happiness in the world.

Aloof and fiercely loving the unattainable, I was simultaneously full of love for many people and also allowed myself to live out this love — sometimes, briefly and fiercely, sometimes faithfully, long, and weakening.

Everyone finds out for themselves what is right.

Our world is changing, and we humans are changing, including in our relationships with each other. Whereas the post-war generation was mainly concerned with functioning, re-building, and security, today individuality is at the forefront. Families are falling apart, we are scattering and isolating ourselves. There are so many influences, information, and opinions to consider.

How can all an individual person's facets suit me? It's an impossibility. Then there are my bad experiences with animalistic possessiveness, which isn't good for anyone. A friend said: "Why should I have just one boyfriend when I can have many?" Isn't she right? She was. When I think about my experience with possessiveness, guilt isn't an issue, nor is good and evil, because I know about and believe in the meaning behind everything.

If I want to get to the root of the evil in this life, I must dive back into the evil from previous lives. It might be helpful to hear an expert opinion on this, that of a regression expert, because the psychologists and psychiatrists I've interviewed so far probably had no idea about reincarnation. Esoteric nonsense? I know what I've experienced. Myself as Jesus, Mary, and God. Oh, no thanks. Me? That's too much honor, it can't be.

I played the victim, felt a tremendous responsibility, had to make sure that this world kept turning, and that wasn't enough. It depended on me alone whether everything or nothing would win. To be or not to be was the question within me and this heavy responsibility weighed heavily on that cross. How much I suffered. Whether as Jesus, a witch, or beheaded by the guillotine, or as a man put up against a wall and shot in a war. I always stood up for what was good and lost my life for it.

Poor good Billy, the sacrificial lamb?

Did I ever realize on my journey that it is also possible to survive as a winner? Whoever saves themselves saves the whole world? Maybe it's just as true the other way around. If a person wants to heal themselves, they actually have to save the whole world in their mind. After all, what is the point of having a healthy body if there is no longer any earth to walk around on as a human being?

Madness, psychiatry, insane asylum. My fellow human beings had a hard time with me in those days. Who is supposed to understand something like that? As shared earlier, while working as a nurse in a psychiatric ward, I'd met two people who believed they were Jesus.

We have the wonderful universal subconscious in which all experiences are stored. So I don't know if my radio-like brain has simply recalled the experiences of others or if I've actually experienced what I remember in other lives. Fortunately, I was allowed to let my madness run wild on an island in the sea and have only been sedated with drugs once.

STEPS

I have to think about Hermann Hesse at this point because his poem "Steps" (in German *Stufen)* reflects so well what I've practiced for years in order not to run the risk of getting stuck in a monotonous daily grind.

I build a life for myself and when all is safe and settled, just before I can get used to it or put down roots, I want a new one.

The adventure beckons. The beauty of setting off is that I reduce my possessions to the essentials. And time and again, I also reduce my being, shedding obstructive fears and patterns of behavior. Like an onion, I peel off layer after layer, getting closer to myself, to the core. Thus pared down to essentials, I begin to build a nest again, to explore my surroundings and the people around me. Sometimes I struggle, but I know that it's my worse self that wants to slow me down, the acquired, comfortable creature of habit — a lamb. My nature is like a river that just must go on, then pour into the sea. And there I can find peace for a while, until I can't see or enjoy the beauty any longer. Then I let myself be lifted into the air, live the other life again. Work, earn the means to get by, visit a few doctors, get help if I need it.

1998 in December: "Oncogenic HPV infection of the cervix uteri." I was advised to have another operation "as progression cannot be ruled out."

A dream on the subject: First I was traveling, all my luggage was stolen, found myself with nothing in no man's land, then at the doctor's, who grumbled to me that I shouldn't take myself so seriously, others were even worse off. I was a guest of a couple I was friends with. The woman had just miscarried and I didn't care. I picked up the fetus — a creature as small as a sparrow, managed to breathe life back into it, stroked and cared for it, and it thrived and became a little dog.

In Berlin, I can't escape the news:

On December 16, 1998, the USA attacks Baghdad by air strike, China and Germany do not agree. We are advised to: "Prepare for the worst!"

England supports the USA.

World War III threatens again and Nostradamus is pulled from the bookshelf ... The end of the world at the turn of the millennium.

I'm trying to recover so I can bring life into this world one day, while at the same time, the citizens of the world are at war with each other, not realizing that there are only losers on all sides in war. My gynecologist advises me to find a partner, have lots of sex, give notice at work, and enjoy life, because it's short. He offers me his help, a kind of certificate: cancer, mental stress, expected recurring absences due to illness. I get a yellow certificate of incapacity for work and arrange another operation — at the beginning of next year.

On January 6, 1999, I go under the knife again and hope that my doctor will be able to help me. Normally, the uterus would have to be removed. Fortunately, my gynecologist has now become a friend and accepts my strict no to this. He will try to preserve my ability to become a mother.

January 1999: There is still one centimeter of cervix left, excised and soldered. Thank you. I dream that I'm standing in a burnt clearing in the forest and a stork comes along and circles me twice. It's interesting how the psyche processes things in life.

Attend a Greek course at night school for three months so that I can communicate in my adopted country. Keep my job until my wishes are clearer. A month's breather on Crete is planned.

March 1999: As I countered my inability to commit and my dream of the unattainable right one with a rather wild love life, I often had myself tested for AIDS. This doctor also almost became a friend. He was planning to emigrate to Vietnam, and I asked if I could join him.

Why not?

So, on his advice, I had all the application documents translated into English and brought them to him. His brother would "go over" in April, take our documents with him and make enquiries on the spot. I shouldn't dwell on it. Good. There's no harm in trying something new.

END-OF-LIFE CARE

Four hours after I'd spoken with him about life after death, the first man who proposed to me died. He was already 100 years old and suffering from cancer. Gently, and with eye contact between us, I'd shared with him in his last hours:

"Do you know that death is not the end? You know Albert Einstein and his insight that energy isn't lost, right?

Your mind, your thoughts, your consciousness are made up of electromagnetic vibrations. They are not bound to matter and so they aren't subject to the laws of space and time.

You, that which makes you, your soul, is immortal and it is up to you to free yourself. Let go when you can no longer bear the pain, when the misery becomes unbearable! Don't be afraid, death is just one step.

It would be utterly pointless to spend your life learning and growing only to die with this wealth of experience. Your spirit has grown, as has your heart. Our wealth of experience of the world also wants to grow. This is why we are here, I think, living our different lives.

I've experienced that help is waiting at the gate from those who were most important to you when you were alive. Who do you think will be waiting for you there?

Have a good and safe journey. Take care!"

I suspect many of you are going, "Why is Billy telling me this story now?"

I'll tell you, it's because when I spoke with my patients about death like the example above, it seemed to take away the fear of finally letting go,

I can talk people to death. And that's why people are happy to leave the end-of-life care to me.

ZEST FOR LIFE

I'm back at the sea. Shortly before I arrived here, three young Albanians were deported to their home country to be sent to war. One of them was a friend of mine — a very quiet guy, never angry. He now must go to a war that he didn't want. Like a pawn in a game that others are playing. His life is at risk and will be sacrificed if necessary. He has no choice; his life doesn't seem to belong to him. He's powerless and so am I in the face of war.

Sometimes I'm ashamed of how lucky I am to live in such a safe and rich country. In Germany, I can earn good money and travel wherever I want.

Like now.

Unfortunately, rights and goods are very unfairly distributed around the world, and I can understand anyone who leaves their shattered homeland to get a better piece of the pie elsewhere. I've done the same.

Since 1993, I've had uterine surgery year after year, and I thought my life was likely to be short-lived. I was supposed to spice it up, give it meaning, live it to the full.

My job is history and I no longer have an apartment. I've saved ample amounts of money and have a desire to travel, but no destination. My roof over my head is a tent on the beach, my belongings have been reduced to the bare minimum.

I'm on Crete to find a destination and I find it in person who has the same name as I do. I'm invited to come to South Africa. The inviter leaves, I fall in love once again with a brotherly friend who, for his part, doesn't want to fall in love with me. It's like a song I heard:

"Hans loves Betty, But Betty loves Joe.
None of us will ever know real joy."

JOURNEYS

On Crete in August-November 1999.

From November 1999 to January 16, 2000, I went back to work as a nurse in Berlin. Then I booked myself a ticket to South Africa, only to then have my ob-gyn inform me that I was not cured. I would have to have surgery again. The really, finally last operation took place on January 5, 2000. On January 17, 2000, I fasten my rucksack and fly to Johannesburg, South Africa. I'm picked up and am the guest of close friends of Nelson Mandela.

I soon land in Rustlers Valley, a valley in which a permaculture center has been set up, run by young people from all over the world together with locals. Everything is recycled and returned to the cycle. There are a number of self-awareness courses here and the guests bring money into the coffers. I work in the team in exchange for room and board, make friends, and am in good hands for a while. A friend takes me to Durban. On the way, I feast my eyes on the scenery and am thrilled to see exotic animals living free.

I also see that white South Africans live in high-security compounds. I learn that every member of my friend's family has a car. No white person dares to go out on foot in Durban.

To extend my visa, I take a trip to Lesotho. I'm met in a friendly manner everywhere, although I'm the only person with a different skin color far and wide.

Up there in the mountains, that strange feeling that I had once before in India creeps up on me again. So foreign in a foreign land, I feel like an intruder, playing a guest role in other people's lives, visiting a world where everyone but me seems to have their place and their task.

South Africa has a different calendar, and I experience a huge festival at the turn of the millennium. Several bands play their hearts out. The valley shakes with thousands of dancing feet — an unforgettable experience!

After the wanderlust, I am now homesick. I'm no longer at home in the East, but West Germany hasn't yet become my home either. My chosen profession is good for a short time, but quickly leads to exhaustion ... two people responsible for 50 patients, medical care, nutrition, helping people use the restroom as long as they can still walk, if not, changing diapers or handing out incontinence medication ... getting people out of bed and back in again, doing laundry ...

There is hardly any time for compassion and conversation. My own healthy eating falls by the wayside. Where should I go? I no longer have an apartment; all bridges have been burned.

April 29-June 28, 2000, Crete
June 28-July 5, 2000, Berlin
July 5- July 19, 2000, Crete
July 19-28, 2000, Berlin
July 28-August 4, 2000, Crete
August 4-September 22, 2000, Berlin
September 22-October 21, 2000, Crete
October 10, 2000, Arrival Berlin

At the end of June 2000, I felt so liberated, but now I'm already quite close to madness again, have strange feelings in my belly, and a child's voice in my ear: You are not solely responsible for yourself.

My belly symptoms could mean cancer or pregnancy. But

I haven't had sex, yet a little voice told me I was pregnant. Of course, no one believed me. And since I'd been disappointed or fooled so often in the past, I was no longer sure of myself. I went to Berlin and had it confirmed. I wasn't pregnant.

Disappointed, homeless, without any ties, I met someone I used to love on Crete, reconnected with him to say goodbye, because he wasn't the one I was looking for.

Now, of all times, I actually got pregnant and that was the best thing that could have happened to me at that moment in my life!

REVERBRATIONS

I'm actually surprised at how my love life presents itself to me. Like a butterfly, I fly from flower to flower and am ... already gone again, flying onwards, never to arrive, always on the move, preferring to be one with everything than alone as a couple. Alone with my very own story, like each of us, until I felt the need to share and wrote this book.

POEMS, RANTS, SERIOUSNESS, FURY, AND HUMOR

THE JOURNEY

In mysterious ways,
each one travels their days
along own paths, courses
crossing, intersecting as they may,
but arriving alone, themselves to stay.

Yet each one journeys on anew,
hoping, wanting to become two,
that fuse, becoming one.
Dog and cat, man and man,
woman and woman, woman with man,
long ago, all were...one.

I believe:
We are one.

COIMING AND GOING

Peter (the rock), brother, my own
has become a rock-solid, magic stone,
only that is not true.
When he left, I thought
my heart was breaking in two.

Until he began fishing for me
between my wakefulness and dreams.
Letting go of him, so impossibly hard.
No longer seeing him, yet
missing him eternally, scarred.

If only he were still alive.
I cling to him still, cannot thrive.
Never was I so lost, so bereft
than after my beloved brother's death.

We must comprehend
and not forget all comes to an end.
Otherwise, our lives we waste, expend,
never comprehend the tide turns, bends,
never to truly know,
life's ebb and flow
where one comes, while another goes.

BOREDOM

I give boredom a pass.
It's not in my gene pool.
I'd rather skip that class,
and will not be a fool
or a gate,
though often, alas
boredom seems to await.

I try to make good times
for all the others I just find
when our wanderings entwine.

And sometimes, often actually
I perceive people suffering, terribly.
All shared, joy — and pain,
is not in vain,
only half the weight
or half so light,
forever the worries abate
lose their might.

This girl I know believes
I just flit and fly.
How right she sees,
because fleeting, that's me.
One goes, so another can come by.

Hey Mr. Fisherman,
how deep is the water there,
feet getting wet and wetter,
I'm a sea goat, but body of a fish
stay forever in water, that's my wish.

I'm no longer really healthy
but also, not totally ill.
Still alive, that's the main thing,
thankful this is the universe's will.

So, I write to Earth's Mother
rooted firmly in faith and trust
that I will be found by the other,
as my search for them is dust.

ME, SELF?
ONE?

MIRACLE MAKING

So very many of my life events,
border on miracles, that's just how it tis.
Not madness, mania, or arrogance,
I just love life, the endless dance.
Dancing, now that is honest expression,
the censor confused, can't pay attention.

Only bitter tears, sweet nothing words?
There must be more, or so I've heard,
and believe it is true, definitely, clear.
After repeated pondering, in sadness or cheer,
pensively, or merrily revealed, my observance:
the answer to the riddle lies in balance.

Everything repeating, cold and heat,
leaves of autumn falling, rain becoming sleet,
and then already once more, back to ice,
only to thaw anew, kissed by a warm bride.

This brings me to battles between the sexes,
which truth is more real, this question vexes,
is the sun a woman, the moon a man?
That can't be so, is how it feels.
It doesn't matter, surely, it's no big deal —
he sun, she moon, she sun, he moon,
human thoughts, living in basement gloom.

But never, never is it ever too late,
for the Earth's turn, for it to rotate,
miracles happen, have happened to me,
trust in oneself, that's what sets free.
Not always believing all that you hear,
words often destroy truth, muddy the clear.

So, I'm quiet, just absorbing sounds,
until very, very softly, I'm humming a round.
At dawn enchanting birds, chirping their songs,
I don't want sleep now, wakefulness prolongs.
I want to do so much in and around my nest,
making magic, wild, untamed, afterwards, rest.

Solely in peaceful quiet lies power and strength's source.
Body and soul — slacken in sleep, a matter of course.
Through the sea of dreams, wandering without peace
is my soul, searching for yours, loving for better or worse.
Is that perhaps, per chance my curse?

No, not worse, not a curse, but vital and true
Love of life, no this, I'll not rue.
It is — was, and will, be just fine by me.
Happiness is more than luck, this I can see.
Being stupid is not smart,
but smart talking is a deceitful dart.

Anyway, everything is make-believe, pretend,
like just now about not being tired at long day's end.
I go round and round on a never-ending travelling trip,
But when I put myself to bed,
the question, "What is this shit?" pounds in my head.

Perhaps one day someone can laugh or learn
About what haunts me at night as I toss and turn.
Day is in love with night,
How beautiful, and oh how right.

And you? What say you to this tale?
That I was just a windbag, an old chatterbox,
on the way to being skin and bones, that shocks.
Time now for "still-not-eating-much-Annette"
to calm herself down, smoke a cigarette.
Slowly, coughing girl, water is the savior,
douse burning feet, do not waiver.

Water essence of life, its soil,
Those who know this not, must hover or toil
Between the worlds and catch cold
Just like so many who have gone before,
you find them as you wander, and life explore.

Or they will scorch each other's heads,
torturing ears, ending in shreds,
blinding their eyes,
 for the birds — but can't fly.

Maybe you've been watching too much TV?
No, I saw it close enough to me.
They fan your fears — and that's deceit!
They want to sell us good cheer with soft drinks.
I can only tear out my hair, I think.

You can spend lots of money on security measures.
Just you cannot buy that safety you treasure.
Life is, let's be down to Earth honest here,
Life is life-threatening in and of itself, for sure!

And then again, that is also not true,
when examined from another point of view.
We already have been and always will be here forever.
Me, as the Father, Myself is the Son,
and I am the Holy Ghost, all at home, united in one.

I was inside my own mother, actually,
I am also her mother, like this, exactly.
Strange, perhaps, just my guts say it is so.
But I'm just I woman, what do I know.

I will never, ever for one second regret
restarting an over and out, trying a reset.
I'd love to have a man, loving, tender, kind,
and a me being able to sleep at his side.

And Mr. Rabbit, honesty I choose.
Screwing is beautiful. The earth moves,
you fall apart, meaning your ego shatters.
This is not bad at all, as thus,
Love speaks to us.
Love needs no kind words, that's very clear.
Love makes sure that we all know:
We are one, always there.

ME

Only one tone in the world's song,
a painter's brushstroke,
One breath of air, a moment long
I am simply me.
Me ... one more being,
a constantly evolving
expression of existence,
my own forbears, ancestors —
and those of many others.
Me ... that is, we, all, one.

All of us are wanderers,
incomparably changeable:
Alone, we show our faces,
somehow different, each one's traces
appear to eyes of other journeyers.
One breath long with no goal
or compulsion to play a role.

Universal sounds and rhythms of the world's heart,
I must feel you tangibly as part
of the lives of other, everchanging beings,
just as they are for me.
If you love life, it loves you.
If I love and live life, I am me, too.

A wanderer along others' paths,
not always, and never with wrath.
Changing, not always clear,
where the light is shining now, here,
and if it's leading me far, or very near.
What then is life's meaning?
That I AM, a being.

That I am,
joy-bringer to my own
and to others wandering on,
an improving, ever-changing
world brush stroke, simply,
ME.

CHILDEREN OF THE MOON

Before evening falls, bright light remains,
moon's children bathed in sunshine.
At night, their shadows invisible chains
whispering I can only be with him, entwine.
Time, an illusion, faded and dim,
those who can spin, already weave
an own web, include a leitmotiv or whim,
doing as one will, can do no harm, I perceive.
The own self, only the own head can think.
Who else can give me so much understanding,
take some steps with me, and do so daring
alone with all — able to stand me, bearing,
fear and frustration tossed to the wind, not fleeing,
leading the way at dawn,
happily waking up limbs, stifling a yawn,
turning around myself so I see
the sun rising, smiling mischievously,
and continue wandering life's course.
Where we are going, I care not.
I'm with me, and that's enough, a lot.

LOVE

The fifth element, the quintessence ...
I thought it must be love.
Love, oil in the gears, a dove,
a higher love, a deeper emotion,
a seemingly wrong construction.
But what do I know, on the run.

Love comes wearing a bizarre disguise.
The real thing, so hard to see, recognize.
Ah, there we have the moving, instinctive drives,
I mistake them at first for true love's vibes.
A great desire to "must have" then follows,
we find ourselves in animal roles,
blinded by possessive rage.

And then, tangible alarm. This is not good.
Suffering and fear of loss drive us, skewed,
jealousy and beatings, dumb. We're screwed.

MARRIAGE PROPOSAL

You're my happiness, heart, and life — my all,
May I cling to you forever — love eternal.
Love me, too, please, I need you so,
because through life alone, I cannot go.
I'm not fond of standing on my own two feet,
and back-breaking work? No, thanks, will keep my seat.
Could it be that you are so wonderfully stupid and naive
that you'd gladly bear my burdens, carry my cross for me?
Therefore, may I dare to go down now on one knee,
request your hand in marriage, holy matrimony?
Or, alternatively, can I just grab your tits?
Beware, if another guy looks at you, I'll rip him to bits.
And you, stupid bitch, will feel my fists.
Marry me, and take the hits.

The poem "The Grass" by Johannes R. Becher — and its line "I bow down to you, oh grass," inspired me to write the following poem:

254

THE RESPECTFUL BOW

I bow down to you oh stones,
from teensy-tiny, to massively grown,
white, black, multi-colored, too,
I pick you up wherever you're found,
and bow to you, down to the ground.

Then in good cheer, I stand up once more,
see stars above to wonder at and adore.
Now I can, and I must stand straight and tall.
Bowed down, I'd never see dear stars at all.
Full reflection on stars' glory and tracks,
requires us humans, though, to lie on our backs.

This I do gladly and with such frequency,
I'm a starlet myself now, get an eyeful of me.
Gazing at stars, the message I've read,
"You all were once stars, too." That's what it said.
Or in the future, stars, that's what all shall be.
Who can know with any degree of certainty?
It is all show, false light, make believing,
space, time, our very existence, our being.

I bow down before you, oh wood,
show my particularly pride in you, as I should.
I've seen tall-standing trees in deaths throes,
so very sad, yet somehow beautiful to behold!

When wind rages, and wood's branches and twigs break,
I collect them and they cook for me in the fire that I make.

I bow down before you, oh fire.
Even though at times, you burn so wild, so dire,
you bring warmth and give me light.
Otherwise, I cannot see in the dark of night.

I bow down before you oh food,
forgetting about you is never good.
Then those who do not eat, have not long to live,
and will have no joy in the light the fire gives.

I bow down before you, oh joy.
oh majestic spark, godly envoy.
With joy, each day I appreciate,
gladly let myself from you intoxicate.

I bow down before you, oh water.
When I am dry,
you are wetter,
I dive into your embrace,
swim atop your face,
Heavenly alive — a drop in the human race.

I bow down before you, oh life!
All you do and give so I survive,
become the Billy I am now, today,
Billy with love inside, my way,
for creatures great and small,
for infant and ancient, short and tall,
from feverish heat to deadly cold,

for every being I behold,
even the paved road
I bike upon, life supporting my load.

I bow down before you, oh wheels.
the wheel of fortune,
I mean now, and so often.
This wheel I can turn.
And as you know, you can create,
be the master of your very own fate.

I bow down before you, oh death.
I see red.
Death is dead!
Yet, I can still speak with my dead,
pruned from life's tree, spirits in me, instead.
How wonderful that is, great pleasure,
It's said we are— such a treasure,
always here — forever.

You, you, death!
Love I saw the very first time
I looked into your eyes — and you in mine.
And that ...
That was so amazingly beautiful,
I almost could not dare to
believe IT, believe in you.

I bow down before you, oh grass,
thinking Johannes R. is not done,
beneath you, grass, he's having fun.

So quickly I will not end, conclude,
I'm midst in a huge swticheroo.
I'm fiddling with the switches,
want to know who believes me, no glitches,
or whether totally alone I must be
in this life movie,
here in me.

(In this very moment, the wind slams the door with a loud bang.)

I bow down before you, oh rubbish and waste!
When I find you, I'm quite still, no haste.
Discovering you, often fills me with shame,
that I belong to the human race, too, take blame.

Finding you, rubbish, litter between all the stones,
sometimes almost makes me cry, with tears atone.
Finding you in and amongst the trees,
is like icy hail flattening all my dreams.

In a moment, I'll start cleaning up,
sorting, straws together, same with coffee-to-go cups.
I'm great at differentiating who belongs with whom,
and don't avoid bending down to pick up litter strewn.

Here, I cannot take a break.
I can and I will tackle this disgrace.
And I do!
Ashes to ashes
and trees to trees.
And please: put cigarette butts in ashtrays!

ir wollen leben!
höre, bewußte
schreiten aus aller
elt und meine
gst wird mehr
d mehr zur
hühslosen Ge-
sheit...
, wir
ben...

Na, und?
Wir werden
immer leben!
und der
Tod
gehört
schon
immer
dazu

HERE AND NOW

I can continue my metamorphosis today or do it tomorrow.
So might as well be doing it now in joy, not sorrow.
Why take a raincheck, from tomorrow's time borrow?
Get it done today, that's the motto.
Why keep putting things off?
Undone too long, they grow moss,
and drive away tomorrow's fun and gloss.

This we know for sure somehow,
life is always only here and now.
Tomorrow could place other troubles on my mind.
That's why I don't borrow from the morrow, steal time.
I want to be free from these daily routines and details,
that vie for my joy in all today entails.
Hey people, paradise is always found
living in the here and the now!

So go ahead, open your eyes real wide,
instinctively, follow life's path, don't hide.
Action! Do what you like, want, say,
so is fine, so is correct, and very OK.
Give your own life its meaning,
if not, it just flows away, so fleeting.
Do, what brings you joy in life, glee,
but no clinging to things, possessively.

All human belongings, the stuff acquired
leads people to worry, days and nights of perspired
fear that robbers and thieves will make off with their things.
That they are wasting their life with angst, they never see.
I no longer want to lose time or face,
by giving anything besides "life now" more space.

Time is precious, don't want to gamble it away,
like so many others do every day.
Postponing dreams to later, someday, maybe
after bedhopping, sexual adventure are history,
but nursing care hasn't yet knocked on their journey.
Then after decades of dreamtime spent making a living,
all the money saved for somedays is trickling,
right into their doctors' hands. No more dreaming.

They gave up on their dreams long ago,
and along the way, wasted their one life's flow.
How sad at the very last minute,
looking back on a whole life of I didn'ts.
Let us please simply do it better,
and live our dreams and life's variety in full measure.

Today only in the here and now,
believe me, total happiness is found.
I started a new life today, just me,
and guess what? Fireworks went off, coincidentally.
Here and now, I am sufficient, enough alone.

I'm done with self-reproach and self-delusions,
projections, and many other stories that are illusions
destroying my joy in me, sowing confusion ...

The ones trying to make me believe that,
only with them, will I have something to laugh at,
their tired, old stories from yesterdays, past.

I don't want to make fun of others,
better to reflect on what's under my own covers.
Self do, self have, no matter sex or gender.
Every person, their own life-creator, path-bender.
No one else can administer your talents,
do what you gladly want for yourself in all moments,
help yourself to still your own longings,
All is for you to do by yourself.

No making it easy on yourself, or rest for the weary
Get that ass in gear, make tracks, dearie.
Expect help from nothing and nobody,
Make yourself laugh, to yourself, be cheery.

THE PATH TO THE GOAL

Not much further now, goal in sight,
Keep calm, be serene, yes that's right.
Remember, being merry and also gay,
never, ever lengthens the way.
With a spirit full of cheer,
every path seems near.
And lovely it is to see,
others seeing you, understandingly.

We have joy, so be blithe.
The riddle's answer does here abide.
The goal is here, so count me in,
together, let's feel free again.
And when our paths do part,
I can watch you go with peace in my heart.

My goal is near, no longer far,
with serenity as my star.
the goal is me, I know now clearly,
'twas not always so, I paid quite dearly.
This time, I'm all in for me,
my companion, joyful serenity.

Fear and hassles, yesterday's news, burdens from others,
no need or use for them, dear sisters and brothers.
Angst and anger are teachers in our lives,

No way I want to cling to them, they cut like knives.
Sangfroid and poise are parts of loving for me,
those who comprehend this, are eternally free.

Neither space nor time in this journey,
just cheerful serenity.

BEING

When I am one with myself, all honest, clear, and true,
then I know once upon a time, I was another being, too,
and will be again another existence
here on Earth, or elsewhere.
If here — or in heaven's far distance,
wherever at all, no matter the name,
my friend, I am not always the same,
sometimes, I am still not all there, but am sane.

I need something for myself, my essence, my core,
and that is time to realize I like myself, am not in a war.
Love is once again speaking through and in me,
Love, the fifth wheel on the car,
but then again, the fabric that dreams are.

Every cat and every child, or kid
senses exactly when something is truth, or a fib.
Honesty is good and right,
without it our words are nothing, have no might.
Be spontaneous, intuitive,
trusting yourself, that's not naive.

One thing more I feel I must say:
about our feelings, never feel shame.
The heart is trained in every direction,
so in darkness, we find light, the clearing, the lesson,

we're allowed to be angry, and also feel sad,
stumbling around in darkness and seem to feel glad.
Every emotion, each feeling has its place
on the palette of life, vivid treasure to embrace.

THE BUSH

One day, I saw a bush being washed ashore,
arriving from the west after crossing the sea.
I took it in, so it could have a home once more,
and this, I think, makes both of us quite happy.
It has new bearings, an own spot in the great outdoors,
found post-life meaning, reason to still be.
The bush, a beautiful corpse, is now decor
at my makeshift home, camping at the beach with me.

When I light a candle at its feet,
the bush starts glowing so beautifully.
as if it is speaking and wants to greet,
all those beings we cannot see,
and do not know they are watching us.

The bush surely had other dreams,
perhaps a life with roots, bound in ground,
but did not think it would be this lovely thing
the most beautiful of all I have ever found.

Uprooted by wind, transported by river, or stream,
the bush swam to me across the sea,
and I welcomed it with delight, with glee
because this bush was so much like me,
tousled branches
like my hair.

Roots detached, no longer in soil entangled
but at heart, its axes are still stable,
has let go from all, so free, enabled,
almost like it fell out of its world to dangle.
And yet, it is still here for all to behold,
oh beautiful bush, you bring pleasure untold.

AFTERWORD

My wish is that with this book, I've given my thoughts a chance to reach other people — and by doing so, I can take a step out of my own unattainability and speak with those who feel as if my words had something to say to them. Thanks to all who've given me your attention, to life itself, my parents, of course, who made me materialize on the planet, all those I was privileged to have contact with, and for the myriads of wide-ranging, diverse experiences.

Many thanks go specifically to the people who've helped and supported me in the journey to bring this book into the world. These include Elefteria Tsapaki and Stelios Tsapakis, who printed out the rough version, and gave me a first, bound, paper book. Thank you, Eva, for trying to read it, and you, Didi, for sifting and sorting. Thanks to you, Heribert, for formatting and being patient with my continuing education in image editing. Many heartfelt thanks to Gina for translating this book from German to English. Thank you, Susi and everyone who encouraged me, even those who slowed me down, and challenged my belief in myself.

Did it help me to learn to love myself? For sure, it helped me to remember that I've always loved myself anyway.

And everything else too.